M000273622

LITTLE GRAY BASTARDS

BASTARDS

THE INCESSANT
ALIEN PRESENCE

LITTLE GRAY BASTARDS

BASTARDS

THE INCESSANT ALIEN PRESENCE

JORDAN HOFER
& DAVID BARKER

4880 Lower Valley Road • Atglen, PA 19310

DEDICATION

To our daughters:
Hopefully, we are better fathers than ufologists.

ACKNOWLEDGMENTS

Thank you to: Tracie Austin, Tom Bowden, Marla Brooks, William Carpenter, Pat Daniels, Devon Devereaux, Elizabeth Franklin, David Halperin, Anna Hofer, Jana and John Hofer, Jim Holman, Hillary Houha, Dr. David M. Jacobs, Benjamin Jeffries, Dr. Rita Louise, Janet Madland, Jennifer and Mark Madland, John Madland, Mia Madland, Mack Maloney, Kathleen Marden, Chris Olsenius, Linda Olsenius, Valerie Petty, Nick Pope, Alejandro Rojas, Dinah Roseberry, Keith Rowell, Corina Saebels, Reverend Tim Shaw, Pete Schiffer, Denise Stoner, Lady Selah SuJuris, Rick Swope, Kate Valentine, Brett Watson, John Williams, Butch Witkowski, Bryce Zabel, Judy Barker, Hayley Barker, Taryn Barker, Molly Barker, Tessa Barker, Dan Barker, and John Barker. (Apologies to anyone missed.)

PRAISE FOR
LITTLE GRAY BASTARDS

"With its provocative title and striking front cover, *Little Gray Bastards* deserves to become a cult classic with the UFO community. In a field awash with New Age rhetoric, Hofer and Barker certainly don't pull their punches, and cast the alien Grays not as benevolent space people here to save humankind, but as intergalactic bad guys who have infiltrated not just our planet, but our dreams and our very psyches."

—Nick Pope
UK Ministry of Defense UFO Project, 1991–1994

"Jordan Hofer and David Barker have done it again! The fascinating new book *Little Gray Bastards* covers it all. This is a must-read for any ufologist or for any avid UFO reader who wants to learn of the alien agenda, and why the 'incessant alien presence' is not an isolated phenomenon but, in fact, closely related to other paranormal activity....This is a book about victims. Readers will feel the pain."

—Tracie Austin
Executive Producer/Host of *Let's Talk...Paranormal*

"Jordan Hofer and David Barker have written a book that is sympathetic to the abductees and the fear that comes with the knowledge of the aliens' constant presence in our lives, well deserving the title *Little Gray Bastards*. Jordan and David obviously care about what we are going through."

—Corina Saebels
Author of *The Collectors*

"*Little Gray Bastards* pulls no punches and makes no excuses for the Grays' predatory-parasitic behavior. I believe this is a necessary first step toward an end that will eventually require a general rise in human consciousness, rather than military action, to be forever rid of this extraterrestrial race."

—Ed Komarek
Author of *UFOs, Exopolitics and the New World Disorder*

"Jordan Hofer and David Barker take you on an adventure deep into the heart of UFOs and alien abductions. Instead of hearing about these phenomena third hand, you get to meet the people who have had these unexplained experiences and relive their often terrifying nightmares with them."

—Rita Louise, PhD
Author of *ET Chronicles: What Myths and Legends Tell Us About Human Origins*

"*Little Gray Bastards* is both concrete and speculative. Barker and Hofer complement each other. Barker lays out the long, lifetime involvement of the Heriot family with 'the phenomenon.' Hofer provides much of the philosophical, moral, and academically informed speculation about what it all might mean. Barker's odd, but truthful, story provides the grist for ufologist Hofer's opinions, and Hofer delivers. Yet, he makes clear that his is no ivory-tower speculation. He's not above the fray. Indeed, we all seem to be involved at some level. No wonder governments don't want to tell the people!"

—Keith Rowell
Oregon MUFON Assistant State Director

"What makes this book valuable is that it is not simply a book of case histories or anecdotes about those multidimensional/interdimensional soul-scavenging planet-hoppers known in ufology as the Grays. David Barker and Jordan Hofer make perhaps the most essential point about these terrible twerps: that their presence on our planet is extremely closely related to psychic phenomena, ghosts, poltergeists, near-death experiences, out-of-body projections, as well as the UFO mystery. They are pushing the alarm bell to what is really happening in our New World so that the Little Gray Bastards do not become our all-powerful, uncaring, vampiric Gray Masters."

—Brad Steiger
Author of 180 books on UFOs and the strange and the unknown

"If you are just now bravely stepping out to explore the seemingly never-ending circle of UFOs and alien abductions, Hofer and Barker have listed many other titles for you to indulge in. They have also offered areas of history to explore and endless possibilities for the reader to do his or her own research on the topic regarding these 'visitors.' They have opened the door for readers to study, research, and discover what their own conclusions will be…who will fit the final piece of this earth's greatest of puzzles neatly in to place?"

—Denise Stoner
Coauthor of *The Alien Abduction Files*

"Documented human encounters with aliens go back thousands of years. The interaction with these beings is now and has been extremely traumatic in most all cases. *Little Gray Bastards* is a stimulating read on the phenomenon of the Grays. This book has it all, including chilling eyewitness testimony, and is filled with startling witness accounts of one of the most fascinating and troubling facets of ufology. The book encompasses the frightening interactions between human beings and otherworldly beings. This is a researcher's book for certain."

—Butch Witkowski
FFSc Director, Founder UFO Research Center of Pennsylvania (UFORCOP)
Editor, *JAAR: Journal of Abnormal Abduction Research*

Alone, I cannot be—
For Hosts—do visit me—
Recordless Company—
Who baffle Key—

They have no Robes, nor Names—
No Almanacs—nor Climes—
But general Homes
Like Gnomes—

Their Coming, may be known
By Couriers within—
Their going—is not—
For they've never gone—

—Emily Dickinson (1861)

Other Schiffer Books on Related Subjects

A Silent Invasion: The Truth About Aliens, Alien Abductions, and UFOs
Reverend Debra Marshall
ISBN: 978-0-7643-4609-5

Alien Arrival: Salvation or Destruction
Michael FitzGerald
ISBN: 978-0-7643-4763-4

Alien Encounters in the Western United States
Tracie Austin
ISBN: 978-0-7643-4145-8

UFO and Alien Management: A Guide to Discovering, Evaluating, and Directing Sightings, Abductions, and Contactee Experiences
Dinah Roseberry
ISBN: 978-0-7643-4606-4

Other Schiffer Books by the Author

Evolutionary UFOlogy
ISBN: 978-0-7643-4505-0

Copyright © 2016 by Jordan Hofer & David Barker

Library of Congress Control Number: 2015954408

Cover Image © 2014 Devon Devereaux.
Foreword © 2014 Nick Pope.
Authors' Photo © 2014 Mark Madland.
Reptilian-Gray hybrid © 2011 Chris Olsenius,
photograph, © 2014 Mark Madland.
Fragrance 9 oil painting © 2013 Mr. Krister,
photograph, © 2014 Mark Madland.
Eye oil painting on three stacked canvases
© 2014 Mr. Krister, photograph © 2014 Mark Madland.
The Gray digital illustration and photography
© 2014 Mark Madland.

All rights reserved. No part of this work may be reproduced or used in any form or by any means—graphic, electronic, or mechanical, including photocopying or information storage and retrieval systems—without written permission from the publisher.

The scanning, uploading, and distribution of this book or any part thereof via the Internet or via any other means without the permission of the publisher is illegal and punishable by law. Please purchase only authorized editions and do not participate in or encourage the electronic piracy of copyrighted materials.

"Schiffer," "Schiffer Publishing, Ltd. & Design," and the "Design of pen and inkwell" are registered trademarks of Schiffer Publishing, Ltd.

Designed by Matt Goodman

Type set in Times New Roman, Meltdown, Chills & Trade Gothic

ISBN: 978-0-7643-5005-4
Printed in China

Published by Schiffer Publishing, Ltd.
4880 Lower Valley Road
Atglen, PA 19310
Phone: (610) 593-1777;
Fax: (610) 593-2002
E-mail: Info@schifferbooks.com

For our complete selection of fine books on this and related subjects, please visit our website at www.schifferbooks.com. You may also write for a free catalog.

This book may be purchased from the publisher. Please try your bookstore first.

We are always looking for people to write books on new and related subjects. If you have an idea for a book, please contact us at proposals@schifferbooks.com.

Schiffer Publishing's titles are available at special discounts for bulk purchases for sales promotions or premiums. Special editions, including personalized covers, corporate imprints, and excerpts can be created in large quantities for special needs. For more information, contact the publisher.

CONTENTS

FOREWORD
—NICK POPE

Of all the images of extraterrestrials, few are as all-pervasive as the "Gray." Popularized by Whitley Strieber's *Communion*, it soon segued out of ufology and into pop culture, becoming part of the late twentieth and early twenty-first century *Zeitgeist*. The eerie, quasi-human face, with its disproportionately large, angled, almond-shaped eyes is instantly recognizable and can be found not just in UFO literature, but in sci-fi movies, and even on T-shirts and coffee mugs. The image is ubiquitous and has infiltrated our lives, but where does science fiction become science fact? Where does imagination meet reality? What if the infiltration involves more—much more—than just an image? *Little Gray Bastards* attempts to answer some of these questions.

With its provocative title and striking front cover, *Little Gray Bastards* deserves to become a cult classic with the UFO community. In a field awash with New Age rhetoric, Hofer and Barker certainly don't pull their punches, and cast the alien Grays not as benevolent space people here to save humankind, but as intergalactic bad guys who have infiltrated not just our planet, but our dreams and our very psyches.

Hofer's central thesis is that the Grays are a dark, malevolent presence, and in a haunting phrase, he describes the book as being "a document of nightmares." Barker zeroes in on the extraordinary and terrifying experiences of a lifelong abductee who he gives the pseudonym "Earl Heriot." These experiences are nightmares indeed. So tight a focus brings a sense of humanity to an inherently inhuman subject matter. This is a book about victims. Readers will feel the pain. Collaborations are always tricky and can sometimes seem disjointed, but this isn't the case here. The material gels together well, in a way that ensures the whole is greater than the sum of the parts.

Little Gray Bastards is a dark book. Themes of death and destruction run through the narrative. In the science fiction classic *The War of the Worlds*, H. G. Wells describes the invading Martians as having "intellects vast and cool and unsympathetic." One gets a similar feeling when reading *Little Gray Bastards*, though unlike Wells, who wrote about an alien invasion with the enemy at the gates, Hofer and Barker tell a darker story, of an enemy that is through the gates and among us, and of a war that is already lost, because the finest trick of the devil is to persuade you that he does not exist. *Little Gray Bastards* may persuade you otherwise.

NICK POPE WORKED FOR UK MINISTRY OF DEFENSE UFO PROJECT, 1991–1994. HE IS THE AUTHOR OF *ENCOUNTER IN RENDLESHAM FOREST: THE INSIDE STORY OF THE WORLD'S BEST-DOCUMENTED UFO INCIDENT*.

PARANORMALIZATION

THE MORE WE THINK WE KNOW ABOUT
THE GREATER THE UNKNOWN
WE SUSPEND OUR DISBELIEF
AND WE ARE NOT ALONE—

—RUSH, "MYSTIC RHYTHMS"

The Paranormal has become a rock star. Ghost hunters, Bigfoot trackers, and UFO hunters have all appeared on television and garnered loyal audiences in the United States. Are we a particularly superstitious nation, or are we observing a cultural reaction to an increased presence of the paranormal in American life? Perhaps this rash of apparent superstition has arisen from the ruins of American scientific thinking. We are a notoriously anti-science culture. But can this Zeitgeist actually account for thousands of UFO sightings each year? Does it necessarily lead to an increase in alien abductions? If we are imagining all of this, then we must be incredibly prone to a mass hallucination that has spanned decades. Is such a psychological event even possible? Or is the simplest answer to the question of UFO and alien abduction phenomena the one that many of us suspect from our shared experiences? This is all real and it is happening right now. Whether acknowledged as true or not, these strange experiences have become the new normal of the paranormal in everyday life.

Another fact has emerged in ufology: UFOs and aliens are not isolated phenomena, but are closely related to other paranormal activity, including psychic abilities, poltergeists, near-death experiences (NDEs), out-of-body experiences (OBEs), astral projections, extrasensory perception, lucid dreaming, and automatic writing; even Bigfoot appears to spring from the same source of high strangeness. The common denominator that relates all of these phenomena into a singular normalized field is found in the expression of dreams and originates in death.

The truly intriguing reality is that, whether imagined or not, UFOs and aliens are not going away. If anything, there has been a rise in these phenomena. As much as our government denies their existence and mainstream science ignores the evidence, the aliens have maintained an incessant presence among us. They are not going away and they are not leaving us alone. The little Gray bastards have other plans for us.

LITTLE GRAY MASTERS

I continue to reject the attractive notion of the Grays as a fellow moral species, just as society itself must admit that the most powerful humans on the planet care less for us in the masses than they do a hangnail. The majority of us are victims to two, possibly conspiring, alien forces. Between the sadistic pleasures of the Grays and the callous lack of human sympathy shown us by corporations and governments, we find ourselves facing down enslavement and extinction. Our clarity of the situation must not be consternated by the Grays, who promise us worldwide human spiritual evolution, or by the elite ruling class, who assures us fair prosperity while selling us a catastrophic future under their insatiable greed. Is it mere coincidence that the Grays and the super elite both maintain the relationship of master and slave over the seven billion hapless victims comprising the majority of our species? Evidence exists that the rich and powerful humans, specifically those ruling masters of the military industrial complex, have been conspiring with the Grays, perhaps ever since Roswell, and maybe even with another species, the Reptilians.

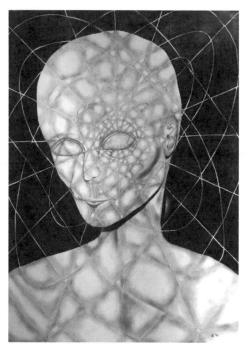

A Reptilian-Gray hybrid. *Graphite on paper, 22" x 30", by Chris Olsenius, 2011. Photograph by Mark Madland, 2014.*

Many UFO conspiracy theories focus on deception from the government, which most certainly exists, but if we want to get to the heart of the alien conspiracy, we should look to the super-rich ruling elite class. At least some of the elite were collaborators with the Nazis, such as IBM and Coca-Cola's infamous Nazi orange soda Fanta. I have no doubt that many of the ruling elite are collaborators with the Grays, a species I have referred to before as "Space Nazis." Between the military industrial complex and the ruling elite, this new exopolitical arrangement is hidden from the American public, just as the Nazi collaborators were primarily silent after the United States declared war on Germany.

Whatever the reality of the situation, I am still far more interested in revealing the "ecstatic truth" as opposed to the "truth of the accountants," as film director Werner Herzog defines them. Only through a strong narrative can any story be fully appreciated, and the alien presence on Earth is no exception; in fact, such an instance of high strangeness positively demands the writer to marshal all of his forces in presenting a comprehensible presentation of the true incomprehensible situation.

The "true situation" is difficult to discern, obviously. The Grays are notoriously deceptive and the UFO and alien phenomena are extremely complex, filled with almost unbelievable accounts of alien contact. When I became a UFO researcher, there were several phases I passed through.

STAGE ONE began with the dawning realization that UFOs are very real objects that can be seen, photographed, tracked on radar, and whose presence sometimes leaves behind trace evidence, such as higher-than-background radiation levels, electromagnetic effects, and changes to plant physiology.

STAGE TWO occurred when I asked the question, "Who or what is flying these craft?" Ufology presents thousands of cases of abduction by alien beings, and most are by the Grays. At this stage, I accepted the evidence of alien abductions and the Grays themselves.

STAGE THREE then begged the question: "What are they doing here? Why are they abducting people?" Opinion varies widely on this point. Human reproduction appears to be their primary interest, with the creation of pale Gray-human hybrids with wispy light blonde hair and intense blue eyes.

STAGE FOUR demanded a larger galactic view of the situation. Not only do the Grays exist, but they are competing and at war with other apex galactic predators. As if one alien species were not enough, abduction reports over the years have reported a wide variation of extraterrestrials interacting with humans. But the reports always inevitably return to the Grays. It is possible that the other beings are merely screen images projected by the Grays to frighten and confuse us. Quantum physics offers the possibility of an infinity of universes, opening up interdimensional travel between universes, and confounding the nuts and bolts physical reality attributed to aliens and UFOs. Once I fell down this rabbit hole, Alice-style, there was no turning back. Further research dominates the focus of my everyday reading, even if the book is a fictional account of UFOs and aliens. The only other discipline that has so entranced and captured my imagination, ultimately changing my worldview, is the study of human evolution. In short, ufology is addictive and, as a UFO researcher, I can only come to terms with this addiction by feeding it.

STAGE FIVE introduced government conspiracy theory to my UFO studies, including above top-secret documents, the Men In Black, and suspected surveillance by government agencies and private contractors.

STAGE SIX inevitably followed with a heavy dose of paranoia, which is either an appropriate reaction or else a confounding distraction; either way, I am admittedly paranoid that the aliens are watching, that they are indeed an incessant presence.

Recently, my daughter saw another UFO while traveling south along Interstate 5: she sighted a shiny, red, star-like object in the west move upwards at about a 45° angle from south to north in approximately three seconds. After describing the object on MUFON's online sighting report, the Assistant State Director of Oregon MUFON, Keith Rowell, wrote her back, explaining that the object is unidentifiable, and thus a UFO. As an investigator, that is as far as Mr. Rowell was able to go with the information available. But I sincerely believe a connection exists between the writing of this book and my daughter's most recent sighting. Did the Grays show off their craft for my daughter as a warning to me?

I suffered (and I mean suffered) from nightmares for weeks after her sighting. One night, I screamed and moaned loudly enough for everyone in the house to hear. My daughter, who was still awake at the time, came to check on me. She was frightened, "fearing the worst," she said (i.e., that Grays were tormenting me). Despite her fear, she bravely came to my bed and comforted me. She told me later that I had said I was not alone in the room, and that was the reason I'd cried out. She also told me that I said this had happened to me in the past when I was a kid. I have no memory of telling her any of this, nor do I remember having these dreams as a child. I am now considering hypnotic regression.

After these nightmares, I became quite anxious and asked a paranormal group on Facebook for assistance. The one comment I received allowed me to figure out how to create a psychic shield to protect myself and family from alien interference or abduction. I have also added a protection prayer to the Archangel Michael that researcher Dinah Roseberry uses for extra protection against paranormal forces that may want to harm her (Roseberry 2014). The psychic shield was already strong and now, after strengthening it further, I hope my home will be protected better than my dreams imply. No one else in the house has complained of nightmares or other disturbances. Mine, however, have persisted. Strange disturbances continue as this book is written and put together. The other night I heard a loud tapping on the window near my head. I got up and turned on all the outside lights, looked around and saw nothing unusual, so I went back to sleep. And just now, at this time of writing, I saw a Gray in the hallway, peeking into the room, grasping the doorjamb. Hallucination?

No. Assigning mundane explanations to high strangeness is a massive mistake of perception and ontology. I suggest the following three terms for the absurd denial of UFO phenomena we have heard from debunkers over the last several decades:

1. "Swamp-gassing" is an inaccurate ad hoc natural explanation for UFO phenomena.

2. "Weather-ballooning" is an inaccurate ad hoc technological explanation for UFO phenomena.

3. "Sleep-paralysising" is an inaccurate ad hoc medical explanation for UFO and alien abduction phenomena.

The danger of assigning mundane explanations to UFOs and aliens is that the aliens are up to anything but the mundane.

This book covers many strange phenomena, all of which I believe are related in some deeper way than any analysis could reveal. My chapters are intercalary to David Barker's story of Earl Heriot's life with the persistent alien presence. I discuss alien abductions and two new cases that I've investigated, the phenomenon of aliens using artists as communication devices, connections between ghosts and aliens, confusion about ufology, a chronicle of alien attacks, as well as a short conclusion. I have wanted to write with David for well over twenty years. For me, this book represents the realization of a lifelong dream. It is a document of nightmares.

Many strange, perhaps paranoid, coincidences occur when I write a UFO book. I suffered nightmares and "hallucinations" while writing *Evolutionary Ufology*. Now it's happening again, and this time it's not just me in Gray cross hairs but David as well. The Grays are totally in control. I have not been sleeping well. I have been confused and frightened. A similar feeling was present on the set of *Close Encounters of the Third Kind*, a paranoia that there was an "invisible force," as actress Teri Garr explained (Beckley 1992), "I kept looking around and thinking, 'There must be greater forces than us here, and they want us to do everything their way!'"

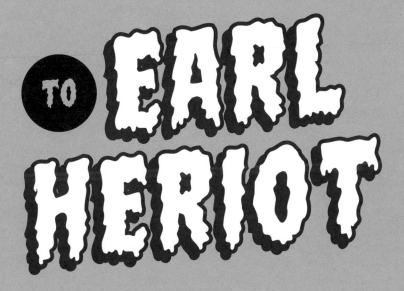

TO EARL HERIOT

My friend Earl Heriot (pseudonym) never discusses UFOs with anyone other than close friends or family members. He is keenly aware that, in our culture, those who admit they "believe" in the existence of UFOs are considered at the very least to be eccentric and, at the worst, nut cases.

As a professional in a technical field, Heriot can't afford to have management wondering about his rationality and judgment. His employer counts on him to see situations clearly, to objectively analyze complex information, and then to make good decisions. He can't have the higher-ups at work doubting his sanity.

Those of us who know him well realize there's another side to Heriot that is never seen by the people he works with. He's a self-described "experiencer."

"Throughout my life," says Heriot, "I've had a number of paranormal experiences. In addition, I have many memories that contain no consciously remembered paranormal aspects, but which have an odd, unsettling feeling to them. These incongruous memories stand out, for some reason, and have an aura of mystery to them. Some of this mental debris involves UFOs and aliens,

17

while other pieces do not, being examples of paranormal activity, episodes of psychic ability, and other bizarre experiences. Put simply, my mind is populated with strange images and thoughts that I can't explain away, and yet I'm a sane, rational person who leads a normal, productive life grounded in everyday reality."

Having a history of mysterious, unexplained and bizarre memories, mental images, and dreams is symptomatic of people who are "potential" or "latent" (meaning unidentified or unconfirmed) alien abductees. He laughs nervously when I point this out to him.

"Don't remind me," he says.

"Would you consider undergoing hypnotic regression in an attempt to get to the bottom of these memories? Hypnosis can recover information buried in your subconscious about what actually happened during these experiences."

"No way. I'd rather not know the full truth. The little bit I do know is just enough to scare me off from wanting to learn more. Besides, there's a kind of beauty to the mystery of not knowing, really knowing, your own history. I kind of like that. I can ponder these experiences, daydream about them, wonder what they might mean, but I never have to really face them and deal with them. I don't have to resolve them. I can leave them vague and half-formed in my mind."

I try another tact on him. "Do you consider yourself a possible abductee, one who only partly remembers experiences that you've been programmed to forget?"

He stares off into space for several seconds, considering what he will say about this. "No, not quite. What I do consider myself is someone who has been aware of an alien presence in the world for most of his life. The reality of aliens has always been a given to me, something I never really questioned. I 'feel' them out there, but I don't want to admit that I've had encounters with them. On the other hand, I have had a lot of weird experiences, and being an abductee would explain that."

Heriot views his own history from the perspective of an open-minded observer of the UFO phenomenon. As an "occasional ufologist" taking the same approach, I think it would be useful to lay out these experiences in as much detail as I can and see if any patterns emerge or if I can gain insight into what's behind all this strange matter in Earl Heriot's life.

Earl agreed to be interviewed for this book as long as he could maintain his anonymity through use of a pseudonym. I asked him to tell me about his experiences and memories in chronological order, to the extent possible, starting with the oldest ones and working his way forward to the present. For many of his anecdotal memories, Heriot doesn't have an exact date or even an exact year. However, he can usually assign them to a decade, based on circumstantial details and his impression of how old he was at the time they happened.

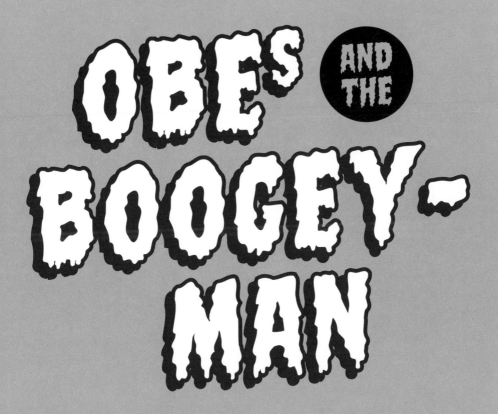

CHAPTER ONE

OBES AND THE BOOGEY-MAN

Heriot's first consciously recollected paranormal experience happened about 1951, when he was around three years old. He has other memories predating this experience, but they're mundane in nature. At the time, the experience seemed perfectly natural to him because, as he puts it:

I was too young to know that what happened would be considered by most people as very strange or even impossible.

We had just moved to Los Angeles, into a neighborhood that later became notorious as the site of the 1965 Watts Riots. I was born in Chicago in 1948. In 1950, my parents moved with me and my older brother Bud [pseudonym, or "Rooster" as he likes to be called] to Phoenix, Arizona. We stayed there for a few months while Dad looked for work, and then we moved into a "court-style" apartment complex on East Century Boulevard, in Los Angeles, near the intersection with Avalon Boulevard.

I have fleeting memories of being an infant in Chicago and a toddler in Phoenix and in Los Angeles. My whole world was my mother and father, and big brother. Rooster and I played with a few neighbor kids, but that was the extent of our social life.

Then, one afternoon, two things happened that were very much out of the ordinary. They were so unusual that, by association, I have a clear memory of the hour or so preceding the first strange occurrence. We had been somewhere in the car during the day. Judging from that, I assume it was on the weekend, as my dad would have been at work on any given weekday afternoon. We stopped at a little neighborhood market on the way home. It was near our apartment, the kind of narrow, old-fashioned corner market that was common in the 1950s but, by now, has all but disappeared. I remember it more as a liquor store than a supermarket, long and narrow and crowded with merchandise. I walked in with my father, holding his hand. He bought one or two items we needed. Maybe it was milk. My dad paid at the tall counter near the door, and then we walked out and got back in the car, arriving home shortly after.

Hardly a memorable event by itself, and yet it's etched into my brain because of what happened later, during the late afternoon or early evening. We were inside the apartment, too late for us kids to play outside, and I happened to look at one of the windows. What I saw terrified me. It was a big, ugly, grotesque face, positioned low outside the window, peering into the room at me, just over the sill. It was larger than a normal adult human face, and it was gnarled up like a gnome's."

In 1997, Heriot wrote a short unpublished essay about this and a few other early paranormal experiences. Here's how he described the Watts event in that document:

Sometimes, in the evening, a monstrous face appeared in my bedroom window—big and green and grotesque. A little girl we played with, who lived in the same courts as we did, told me to watch out for the Boogeyman, that he came out after dinner and got children who weren't in their houses. The face in the window was scary...

Back then, he recalled the sighting of a non-human entity as a recurring event, but now, fifteen years later, he only remembers that one, first sighting.

"This was my first encounter with aliens," says Heriot, "followed by an utterly bizarre event that happened on the same evening."

As usual, my mom put me down for bed early, perhaps about 7 p.m. I recall her carrying me into the bedroom, laying me down on the mattress of my crib, saying a few calming words, and kissing me goodnight. Then, she walked away and shut the door.

> As soon as she was gone, a most unexpected and miraculous thing happened. I became as light as a feather and slowly, gently floated up, out of my crib and up to the ceiling in the corner of the room. This remarkable "levitation" took only a few seconds. When I came to rest against the ceiling, I stayed there for a while, my tiny body pressed cozily against the plaster, and then, after I'd been there a short time, I continued to rise again, this time through the ceiling, my "body" passing through the solid matter of the building, and up into the sky, high above the apartment.

Later, as an adult, Heriot heard about the phenomenon of "astral traveling" and viewing his childhood levitation experience in that context, he came to think of it as his spirit or "astral body" leaving his physical body and moving about freely in another dimension. He says he had levitation experiences almost nightly while growing up. It only stopped when he had a frightening experience when he reached college age. One night while asleep and in a dream state, he suddenly became fully conscious and aware that he was astral traveling. Rooster's wife had told him that astral traveling was only dangerous if you woke up while you were out of your body and couldn't get back into your body in time. If that happened, she claimed, you could get stuck there, in another dimension, outside your physical body.

"That freaked me out so much I forced myself never to do it again, and I didn't," Heriot proclaims.

He further says in the 1997 essay:

> I floated up into the corner of the room, and then somehow passed through the ceiling and continued to float up into the sky, going very high, into the stratosphere. The amazing thing is that I could see the blackness of space, the curvature of the earth, the thin layer of glowing atmosphere hugging the planet, high clouds with brilliant white sunlight hitting them, while the sun itself was hidden below the horizon. Whenever I doubt the reality of these experiences, I ask myself how I could have known about that stuff at such an early age, somewhere between two and four years old? I seem to have flown around like this every night until I was about ten. I have memories of seeing the floating astral bodies of other sleepers, of interacting with them in some way.

He explains that until he "freaked out," these almost nightly "dreams" of levitation or astral travel were pleasant, not frightening, and his interactions with other children he encountered in the air were playful. There was nothing scary about these experiences.

Later—much later—he began to sense a possible connection between the grotesque face in the window and the onset of what may have been what is called an out-of-body experience, or OBE. People who see UFOs and suspect alien abductions or encounters also often report OBEs, and the two are often associated events, with the OBE occurring before or during an encounter with alien beings.

"At the time," says Heriot, "I didn't make a connection between the face in the window and later the 'floating in air' experience. The face frightened me, while floating up out of my crib and into the sky was a peaceful, joyful thing that felt perfectly natural because I didn't know I wasn't supposed to do it. I thought all kids flew at night."

A couple of years ago, I asked Rooster about the time he and Earl lived in Watts and if he remembered anything unusual happening there. He did, and it's something about which Earl has no recollection. He says that they were playing outside with a group of kids and one of them threw a ball straight up in the air. In Rooster's words: "It went higher and higher until it was out of sight, and it never came back down. We waited for the ball to fall but, magically, it stayed up in the air. After a while, we gave up on getting it back and moved on to other games."

The Heriot family lived in Los Angles until 1952, when they moved to Lakewood, a nearby suburb. Their house was on Pimenta Avenue, just south of Del Amo Boulevard. Leaving Watts did not bring an end to the presence of aliens in his life. Earl claims that the family continued to have strange experiences at their new home.

"One afternoon in Lakewood," relates Earl, "my parents watched a large UFO hovering motionlessly over the ocean for about an hour. I have no memory of the sighting, but I do remember my parents talking about it later. The little I recall of the story is that the UFO was in the sky out over the Pacific Ocean." Their Lakewood address was about seven miles from the beach.

In early 2014, I asked Rooster about this sighting of a UFO over the ocean. He doesn't remember it, but he does remember another sighting in which he and his parents were in the backyard at their Lakewood home during the day and watched what his mom and dad called "a cigar-shaped UFO." Rooster says it was "high in the sky, directly overhead." They observed the strange object for about an hour. Due to his acute nearsightedness, the UFO only looked like "a speck" to Rooster and he couldn't discern its shape, but his parents could see that it was cigar-shaped.

About this backyard sighting, Earl says, "I don't recall having personally seen this UFO, although I do seem to remember that at some point during my childhood my parents saw a cigar-shaped object, so perhaps these two sightings are actually only one sighting, with me and Rooster remembering it differently."

Rooster has no idea what year this happened, and can't even say if it was in the 1950s or 1960s.

When Earl was in elementary school, he went to a birthday party for a little girl who lived down the street in Lakewood. It was a typical kid's birthday party until something happened that has haunted him to this day. In Heriot's words:

The party began inside the girl's house, with perhaps a dozen children attending, and a few moms overseeing the event. This took place during the day. Towards the end of the party, we were led by one or two adults into the garage. The garage door was lowered, making it dark inside, and a small portable movie screen was set up in front of the garage door. In the middle of the garage were rows of folding chairs, and behind them was a movie projector on a small table. The children all got excited when one of the moms said we were going to watch a film.

What's strange about this otherwise forgettable incident, is that we were told that the information in the film was secret and we were not to talk about it with anyone. I remember nothing else about the party from the moment the film began. Nothing about the film, or anything that might have been said by the adults, or how the party ended. I don't even have an idea of the general subject matter of the film.

Heriot says this is a genuine memory, not a fantasy or a mental image that he may have picked up from the culture. "I always thought it was peculiar, and when I read in one of Whitley Strieber's books that he has strange childhood memories of attending a 'secret school,' I began to wonder if this odd incident in my childhood was somehow related to aliens."

Heriot doesn't remember the names of any of the kids who were at the party, so there's no way they could be located now and interviewed to confirm or deny the secret film showing. His impression is that he was in third or fourth grade when it happened, making the date 1956 or 1957.

One morning in the late 1950s or early 1960s, Heriot's father told him and his brothers that their mother had had a bad nightmare the night before and was very disturbed by it.

Heriot describes the incident thus:

Starting in late 1957, Mom and Dad slept on a fold-out sofa bed in what we called the "Rumpus Room," which was a rec-room or family room at the back of our house in Lakewood. In her bad dream she awoke in the middle of the night to find that the bed was surrounded by a group of little men, as she called them. She was still very upset by this in the morning and my dad had to comfort her for quite a while until she finally calmed down.

Was this an alien abduction or attempted abduction? Heriot says:

I don't recall either my mom or dad suggesting this was anything but a bad dream or that it had anything to do with aliens, but that idea did enter my mind at the time. I don't remember my parents ever talking about this incident with us kids after that morning.

Heriot remembers that a residential street one or two blocks west of Pimenta Avenue had a long, deep trench dug in it at some time in the 1950s. This was probably related to work on a sewer line. He says:

> I saw this trench daily on my walks to and from elementary school. I have a strange mental image of an alien spacecraft nestled down in that trench, and this made me frightened whenever I passed the site.

This is one of three strange memories Heriot has that involve UFOs nestled in pits in the ground. Two other stories of UFOs in pits follow.

During the 1950s and 1960s, the Heriot family took a number of long-distance trips by car to visit relatives back East. Earl thinks something bizarre happened on one of those trips. Heriot can't pin down precisely when or where it happened.

> It's an isolated fragment of memory with no real beginning or ending, just two brief episodes lasting a few seconds each from the middle of the incident.
>
> I'm in a dense forest where there's a small flying saucer resting on the ground in a shallow circular pit. The saucer is bell-shaped and about twenty feet in diameter. The pit is only slightly larger than the saucer and is just deep enough to accommodate the saucer's height. I have a fleeting glimpse of the saucer in its "nest" from about ten feet away, and a memory of being taken to it, but no memory of any alien beings or other humans present. Then I remember later being inside the craft, in a small room that is cluttered with equipment. I'm on a bed or reclining chair that looks kind of like a dentist's chair, and some sort of articulated mechanical robot arm is coming down from the ceiling and towards me. The mechanical arm is thicker at the top and tapered at the bottom, and there's a long, slender needle on the end of it that comes right at my face and enters my left eye. I have no memory of seeing any beings inside the ship and no recollection of what my emotional state was during the event. All I recall is thinking that a needle is not supposed to go into your eye. That's bad!

The third of Heriot's bizarre memories involving UFOs nestled in pits dates from sometime in the 1950s or early 1960s. On weekends, Heriot's family often made trips by car to the Camp Pendleton Marine Corps Base to spend the day with the Potter family. The base is located seventy-five miles south of Lakewood, near Oceanside, on the Southern California coast.

Paul and Mary Potter (pseudonyms) were longtime friends of Heriot's parents. The Potters had two sons, Paul Junior and Gary (pseudonyms). Paul Senior was a chief petty officer in the Navy and the Potters lived in housing on the base. Although Camp Pendleton is a Marine base, there's been a Naval hospital there since 1942, and Heriot thinks Paul Senior probably worked at the hospital.

According to Heriot:

The Potters had an apartment in a housing complex on the base that was in a park-like setting with green lawns. We kids would run and play outside for hours while the adults stayed indoors and talked. Sometimes we wandered off to a part of the camp where there was bare dirt. It had a rough terrain covered with hills and dales. There were also some ruined structures there. My impression is that this place was probably a bombing range that the military used for target practice. I have an odd feeling about that part of the base, an unsettling mental image centering on a big hole in the ground that may have been a bomb crater. My memory associates this bomb crater with a flying saucer hidden inside it.

In January 2014, I asked Rooster if he had any memory of such an area at the base. The only thing he could think of was that he and the other kids once climbed "a really steep dirt hill of about 45°."

"Do you remember what was on the other side of the hill?" I asked.

"No," he said regretfully, "just going up the hill."

About this apparent discrepancy in their respective memories, Earl says, "We could be remembering the same thing, just in different ways. If we are, Rooster's memory of it stops before mine does, because I remember reaching the top of a rise and looking down into that hole. This is associated with the next weird memory I have, the one about some cows in the fog. That one's a much more uncanny memory and is far more vivid."

Late one afternoon in the '50s or early '60s, the Heriot family was driving home along Pacific Coast Highway after visiting the Potters in Camp Pendleton. A heavy fog had rolled in off the ocean, and visibility on the road was poor, only about ten feet. Something odd happened in that fog that seems innocent enough on the surface, but has troubling undertones.

Heriot reports that:

My dad drove along slowly with the headlights on. At some point, he pulled off the highway and into a farmer's field. There was no roadside ditch or fence between the field and the highway. He drove a short distance into the field and then stopped the car. A while later, a small herd of cows emerged from out of the fog in front of our parked car and approached us.

The memory ends there.

I have no recollection of what happened next. I don't know how long we were there before we got back on the road, or how my dad managed to drive away without hitting any cows.

I find this story highly suggestive of an alien encounter that has been camouflaged with a false memory implanted in the mind of the victim by his abductors. There are many cases where suspected victims of alien abduction report seeing cows, owls, deer, wolves, or other animals, after which they have a "missing time" episode. Ufologist Budd Hopkins (June 1931–August 2011) termed these suspicious sightings of animals in strange situations "screen memories." The theory is that aliens may imbed false images in abductees' minds to mask the traumatic experience of being taken captive. The victim is made to forget the actual experience, which is terrifying, remembering only the screen memory, while forgetting everything else that happens until the time they are returned to their normal life.

The story of the cows and the car doesn't really make sense. Would a farmer leave his cows out in a field with no ditch and no fence to prevent them from roaming out onto the highway where they could be hit by cars? That seems highly unlikely.

The Potters also feature in Heriot's next story. In the late 1950s or early 1960s, Paul Senior retired from the Navy and the Potters moved to Lakewood to be near the Heriots.

Sometime in their childhood, Earl and Rooster claim they heard the sound of a UFO buzzing their home. Even though they didn't see a UFO or any other object that might have caused the sound, they firmly believe that what they heard was a UFO.

Like many of Earl's other strange childhood memories, he doesn't remember exactly what year this happened, but believes it was in the late 1950s or early 1960s, at a time when he was sharing the back bedroom of the house with Rooster. Earl's family moved to Lakewood in 1952, the year the home was built. His younger brother, Jerry (pseudonym), was born a year later. For the first few years in Lakewood, Rooster and Earl slept in the front bedroom and their parents and baby Jerry slept in the back bedroom of the two-bedroom house. In 1957, their dad built the Rumpus Room on the back of the house. His parents moved from the back bedroom into the Rumpus Room, Rooster and Earl moved to the back bedroom, and Jerry moved to the front bedroom.

From old family photos in Earl's possession, I've dated construction of the Rumpus Room to between August 1957 and January 1958, thereby establishing that the "flying saucer sounds" couldn't have happened before August 1957. Rooster and Earl shared the back bedroom until 1967 when Rooster married and left home.

In Earl's words, this is what happened:

Over a period of a few weeks, on several evenings, Rooster and I both heard a weird, unearthly sound that resembled the eerie vibrato oscillations of a theremin [musical instrument] in a horror film. On one occasion, it came in from the east, hovered over the house a while, then moved away to the west. Other times, it would swoosh over the house at high speed without stopping. Whatever object the mysterious noise came from sounded like it was low in the air, directly over our house, and as we listened, we excitedly talked about it being one of those flying saucers that were often in the news. I recall looking out the window that faced into the backyard and peering upward to see if I could observe what was causing the sound, but there was no object in sight. From the angle involved, I wouldn't have been able to see anything that might have been positioned immediately above the house, and I knew it at the time, but I looked anyway. We heard this mysterious sound maybe three or four times during that period. The way I remember it, on no occasion did we go outside to get a better view of the sky. Perhaps we were too afraid of what we might see.

This is how Earl describes the saucer sounds in his 1997 essay:

Lakewood had some weird aspects, as well. My brother Rooster and I would lie in bed at night and listen to this uncanny sound...a loud, humming, swooshing noise...we thought it was giant flying saucers skimming over the rooftops. It was bizarre...not like a plane or helicopter.

In January 2014, I asked Rooster about this incident and he also remembers it, but with minor differences. As Rooster tells it, on several nights they heard a "whirling sound that we thought was a flying saucer" coming from the direction of the nearby Douglas Aircraft Plant in Long Beach, where their dad worked for a while as a machinist. The plant was located a little over a mile from their house.

Twice the sound came over our house. It woke me up some nights.

Rooster doesn't know what year this occurred, but he agrees it took place over a short time period "during one summer" and he agrees it was when he and Earl shared the back bedroom. Rooster thinks he and Earl probably moved into that room because their mother's father came to live with them in 1961, and the grandfather shared the front bedroom with Jerry.

A few weeks later, I asked Rooster again about this event and he expanded on his earlier story without changing anything he had already stated. He said that Paul Potter Junior (who by then was living in Lakewood), told Rooster and Earl that he had heard the same weird sound on the same day they did. Then, one week after Paul heard the saucer sounds, there was a TV news story about a UFO spotted over the May Company Department Store in the nearby Lakewood Shopping Center. Rooster says that he, Paul Junior, and Earl climbed up on the Potters' roof (they lived across the street from the Heriots) to look for the UFO, but they didn't see it.

Rooster says the night Earl looked out the window for it, he looked out the other window at the same time, and neither of them saw anything unusual. Their room was at a corner of the house with one window facing into the backyard and a second window facing the next-door neighbor's house.

According to Rooster, he and Earl both yelled, "Let's go outside and look for it!" He claims that Earl went to get the camera off the top of the dresser. The instant Earl picked up the camera, the strange sound stopped. Rooster thinks the timing was significant, as if whoever was in control of the UFO knew the brothers intended to photograph it, and didn't want them to. Earl doesn't remember himself and Rooster deciding to go outside, or that he got the camera, but he doesn't doubt that it's true.

In his retelling of the story, Rooster described the mysterious sound as being "like the noise of a vacuum cleaner combined with weird humming sounds from a sci-fi movie."

Rooster mentioned to me that he'd heard on a radio talk show that antigravity experiments had been conducted at the Douglas Aircraft plant back then, and he speculated that maybe what he and Earl had heard was the sound of experimental antigravity equipment being tested.

Documents have surfaced on the Web that describe antigravity research conducted at the Douglas Aircraft plant during the late 1960s, and some believe it may have begun in the 1950s.

The next of Earl Heriot's "odd memories" is much easier to date. It belongs to a time when he was in the seventh and eighth grades at Hoover Junior High School in Lakewood, in 1961 and 1962.

Thirty years later, in 1991, Earl jotted down some notes about the strange memory that had long puzzled and disturbed him. Unlike most of his earlier memories that suggest the proximity of alien beings but do not overtly feature the physical presence of such creatures, this memory centers around a clear mental image of repeatedly encountering a tall insectoid being that Earl says looked "a lot like a giant praying mantis." Earl first described this event to me in 2014. There was a hidden closet in the school off one of the classrooms. Children were routinely taken to the closet by a teacher, against their will, and placed inside for a period of about ten minutes. Inside the closet was a tall insect-like being that performed some procedure on the terrified child using a small, hand-held device that, to Earl, looked "like an old Bakelite telephone receiver, black and shiny, but it wasn't a phone. It was some sort of electronic instrument that did something to the kid it was used on." The children went into the closet one at a time, kicking and crying and screaming in fear, and came out a few minutes later quiet and subdued. Strangely, he says, no one at the school ever talked about this. Not the teachers, not the students.

> I never mentioned it to anyone, not even my parents. And had I talked, who would have believed me? It sounds impossible, insane, and yet, it happened for about two years. I'm pretty sure that by the time I was in the ninth grade, it had stopped, for me at least, if not for all the kids.

Earl thinks the insect-like being he saw on many occasions was an alien. He's confident it was not a mere fantasy, a figment of his imagination. By the seventh grade, he was thirteen years old and mature enough to distinguish reality from childish make-believe.

I convinced Earl to share his 1991 notes with me. From them, further details emerged about the "praying mantis" incident, details he had forgotten in the twenty-three years since he'd made the written record of the encounters.

In his notes, Earl says the hidden closet was a small oak-lined enclosure built into a wall of the classroom. The teachers forced the students into the room where the insectoid being used "shiny black instruments" (note the plural) that resembled telephones or medical apparatuses. But then he goes further than in his recent telling of the story, describing how he was subjected to intense pain in addition to fear, and suffered from the dreadful feeling that he had been abandoned by the adults.

He describes the alien's face as cold and emotionless, especially its huge eyes, which he calls "limitless" and "probing." The suggestion is that the eyes have the power to penetrate his mind and exert control over him. In his notes, Earl describes these troubling memories as being hidden. They lurk in his subconscious mind, teasing him from the very edge of consciousness.

There's a weird dream described in the 1991 notes that Earl had entirely forgotten by the time he first told me the story. He writes that it's a "recent" dream, so we can date it to 1991. In the dream, he is the mantis alien, rather than one of its many victims. I have to wonder if this isn't an example of the "Stockholm Syndrome" at work, a psychological phenomenon wherein a hostage sympathizes or emotionally identifies with his or her kidnappers as a survival mechanism. The dream provides what may be additional details about the insectoid alien he encountered in junior high school, preserved deep in Earl's subconscious memory. In the dream, he's an insect-like being that is ten to fifteen feet tall, greenish-brown in color, with a segmented body "like a praying mantis." Oddly, he's the subject of religious-like worship by a human group, a cult. He enters a closet full of communications gear and speaks in an alien language into the mouthpiece of an electronic device. It's not clear in the dream what the location is, whether at a school or elsewhere.

In his 1991 notes, Earl writes of an earlier page of notes that had become lost by 1991. He attempts to reconstruct the content of that lost page in his 1991 document. In this reconstruction of the earlier notes from memory, Earl claims the beings he encountered in the school closet were "The Masters." They were always around, keeping a watchful eye on the students and teachers. He speculates that they may have been elsewhere, in other classrooms, in other schools, all across the nation. He even goes so far as to speculate that the parents of the children were aware of The Masters, but were programmed by aliens not to discuss the nonhuman presence. For all he knows, The Masters are everywhere, in offices and factories and homes, wherever people work and live, controlling their helpless human subjects.

Later in his 1991 notes, Earl reveals a shocking scene that he had totally forgotten by the time we first discussed the mantis-in-the-closet memory. One afternoon after school had let out for the day and most of the kids had gone home, he entered his science classroom to find the teacher, Mr. Saltman (pseudonym), stretched out flat on his back on top of a high counter where lab experiments were performed. Mr. Saltman was unconscious. He was completely naked and his abdomen had been surgically opened from the base of his throat all the way down to his groin. The man's skin was pinned back—much like that of a dead fetal rat in a wax tray during a lab dissection—and the internal organs were visible. Earl was understandably shocked by this horrific sight and could hardly believe his eyes. His mind rebelled against the very idea of it. And then he noticed for the first time something else equally shocking about this seemingly unreal situation.

There was another person in the room: a tall, thin figure wearing a green surgical gown. This strange person loomed over Mr. Saltman's body, apparently performing an operation. How could this be? *It's a school,* his mind shrieked, *not a hospital!* And then this person, who Earl assumed was a doctor, turned and stared at Earl and he saw that it was the praying mantis creature from the closet whose eyes were black and piercing. At that point, Earl fled the room and the school in abject horror, struggling to convince himself that he'd imagined the whole thing as a sort of waking dream, and it wasn't true—that it couldn't be.

All the way home, Earl was frightened. The creature's eyes seemed to radiate pure hatred for him. By the time he got home, he had calmed down and decided that the weird event didn't really happen. The classroom had been empty. No Mr. Saltman there, no alien. Just an empty science classroom in an almost empty school.

The following day at school, Mr. Saltman was fine. Was this a real experience that Earl and the teacher had gone through, or was it possibly a screen memory implanted by aliens to hide whatever really happened on that afternoon? But if these things were screen memories (the mantis, the operation), why would aliens use such disturbing mental images to camouflage their real activities? Instead of a tall insect that inflicts pain, why not a smiling school nurse who smells good and gives a shot that hardly hurts? And instead of a naked and gutted science teacher, why not a kindly old janitor pushing a broom in the empty classroom and saying, "School's out, sonny boy"? If these images are screen memories imbedded in Earl's mind by Grays, why are they such frightening images? How does that conceal a memory from conscious recollection?

Earl knows that aliens have been involved in his and other people's lives in unknown ways for a long time. Intimately involved. He feels their tampering has changed him in some way. That the cruelty he suffered at their hands has turned him into what he calls "a freak." His memories may be largely buried, but their impact on his life isn't.

CHAPTER TWO

ALIEN ABDUCTIONS IN THE RAW

The epidemic of alien abductions in the last fifty years is the most significant and terrifying reminder that we share this planet with a species millions of years ahead of us technologically. We might safely state that the modern age of alien abductions began with the Betty and Barney Hill incident in 1961. Since that time and specific instance, the alien abduction scenario has remained largely unchanged in broad strokes. But that early abduction incident, as frightening as it

> "THESE COLD-BLOODED, HEARTLESS 'BEINGS' HAVE BEEN ABDUCTING US SINCE THE AGE OF FIVE, RAPING OUR MINDS AND BODIES AS WELL AS OUR 'ESSENCE.' OVER AND OVER AGAIN, WITHOUT ONE MOMENT OF THOUGHT OF HOW THIS WOULD AFFECT US! 'THEY' ALWAYS SAY, 'WE WILL NOT HURT YOU,' BUT THE SCARS STILL REMAIN TO THIS DAY FROM WHAT THEY HAVE DONE TO US. THESE SCARS ARE BOTH ON AN EMOTIONAL AND PHYSICAL LEVEL."
>
> —CORINA SAEBELS

remains, has led to more intrusive and violent trespasses upon the human person in the decades since. Betty Hill's amniocentesis procedure, and the rape of Barney Hill for his reproductive cells, seem almost genial compared to the alien abductions of the late twentieth century and the early twenty-first. The harvesting of human sex cells and the hybridization with alien DNA is the most common aspect of the alien abduction phenomenon, and it seems now to be conducted at a fever pitch of activity. And unlike Betty Hill's abductors, aliens today are more deceptive and invasive, their motives far more devious than the early contactees' largely positive interaction with aliens in the 1950s.

The Grays still present themselves to us as beneficent space brothers, deceiving otherwise perceptive people with the message that they are chosen ones destined to lead humanity out of its problems and towards some form of enlightened spiritual evolution. This pleasing narrative spin on abduction and rape is a more transparent ruse now that we can see through this deception to the truth of the situation. The Grays are abducting us to hurt us, to lay claim on the most private aspects of our lives. The Grays often present apocalyptic images to abductees, claiming that the taken must return to their lives and somehow stop the concatenation of environmental degradation and the omnipresent threat of nuclear annihilation. The aliens must be acutely aware that our own scientists warn us daily about these threats to our continued existence, ad nauseam. They must also be aware that the abductees who feel emboldened to fight for the survival of our biosphere and our species will have very little influence over the collective destructive activities of mankind. Alien abduction experiencers are already alienated from mainstream culture, even while that same culture admits in anonymous polls to a belief in the existence of UFOs and the activities of those who fly boldly through our skies and take us from our beds at night. The aliens certainly know that this collection of taken individuals, even as a unified voice, cannot possibly bring about a positive awakening in the human mind to act for the benefit of humanity and the global environment. For as long as this beautiful lie has been told to us, the Grays have not used their technology to assist us in our environmental and social problems. The Grays have no empathy for our plight. Sometimes the Grays will help individuals in need, perhaps curing a minor illness; but these spotty reports of individual assistance are certainly designed to foster a false sense of beneficence from our planet's invaders. They appear to be stepping up their reproductive research as if in anticipation of our swiftly approaching demise. Probably millions of individuals are abducted every year, some of them never to return. In addition, human mutilation has joined cattle mutilation as one of the Grays' pastimes.

But the hypotheses concerning our alien enslavement are nothing without the evidence given by specific people who have unwillingly joined the numbers of the abducted. Their personal stories of confusion, terror, and consequent paranoia are the foundation of any wider view of the alien abduction phenomenon. We can now draw on fifty years of evidence and come to the conclusion that our hypothesis of the Grays as malevolent beings is the clear and present reality.

Two of the most persuasive abductees to speak up have been Karla Turner, author of *Into the Fringe*, *Taken*, and *Masquerade of Angels*, and Corina Saebels, author of *The Collectors*. These two strong and tortured women have given ufology a clear picture of the aliens' true intentions concerning abductions: serial rape and lifelong fear.

To my knowledge, I have never been abducted by aliens, but I have had experiences that allow me to empathize with those who have been taken. The most recent event was in fact a practical joke of dubious humor, perpetrated upon me by my closest friends and our children. We were having a sleepover at our friends' house and I was given a room to myself. I fell asleep quickly and slept well until, at 3:30 a.m., I was awakened by a strange clicking noise. I awoke and opened my eyes to see three small Grays standing by my bed. Their faces were all I could see in the darkness. My memory is a little fuzzy, but apparently I scooted away from the Grays, nearly paralyzed with fear, and said, "Oh, God, no! Go away!" Quite a practical joke. My friends and our children had been planning it for weeks. They ordered three Gray alien costumes on Amazon and got the kids up at 3:30 to "abduct" me. They were concerned that I might attack without thinking, so the kids stayed back about five feet from my head. They also entertained the possibility of a heart attack, but deemed it worth the risk. I have to admit, in retrospect of course, that the joke was pretty funny. But it didn't feel funny at the time. All I felt was terror.

ALEXANDER

Consider the following abduction cases of Alexander and Laura, and attempt to find anything positive in the accounts concerning the everyday operations of the Grays. Alexander says:

> I am a thirty-seven year old man, and I have always been a stargazer since I was young. When I was seventeen, I witnessed a UFO in the skies of Washington State just south of Blaine.

As with many abduction experiences, the abductee might have a history of UFO sightings. Sometimes, UFOs seem to present themselves to humans before taking them away. Perhaps the Grays do this to prepare the person for what is to come, even if it is only until years later. More probable is that the person has had an abduction experience, or perhaps many abductions, and the experience has not yet reached a level of conscious awareness, whether a half-remembered dream or else experiences recalled under hypnosis.

> On May 25, 2013, around 2:30 a.m., my family and I were on a road trip from California to Washington and got stranded on the side of the I-5 freeway at night. It was raining and cold and, as we tried to sleep, I saw a bright light coming at us through the front windshield. It was so bright and fast, and then I just went blank. My girlfriend and I awoke in the car the next morning with no memory of what had happened after seeing the bright object.

Here is the classic alien abduction scenario, with the sighting of a UFO or exceptionally bright light and a period of missing time, during which the abductee remembers nothing, in this case, for several hours. Next, the abductee finds evidence of having been the object of some sort of experimentation aboard the alien craft.

> We had strange marks and puncture wounds on our bodies, and when we got home, my girlfriend and I got really sick with a 103° Fahrenheit temperature that, for me, only lasted twenty-four hours. But my girlfriend's illness and symptoms lasted more than a week and she had needle punctures along her spine from upper neck to lower back. I have dark circles, all the same size and shape, on the back and front of my calves and shins and on my upper and lower back. We have not found anything out of the ordinary with our son.

Puncture wounds and strange bruises are direct evidence of an abduction experience, as is the appearance of strange illness. Alexander and his girlfriend both fell ill following their presumed abduction. Interestingly, the child appeared to be unaffected. Whatever tests the Grays were running on Alexander and his girlfriend were obviously meant for adults. But what kind of tests would result in multiple puncture wounds and circular bruises? How are the "strange marks" connected with the abductees' illness?

Fearing that Alexander and his girlfriend might have some unknown ailment, I highly recommended that they see a medical doctor.

"I believe we may have been abducted from our car that night in May," Alexander wrote me. "I recently spoke with a medical professional and was told that I needed a psychological evaluation. My girlfriend's doctor told her that the punctures along her spine were pores and that she imagined everything that happened to us."

The visit to the doctors' offices obviously did not supply Alexander with the knowledge he wanted. Instead of being treated for what he believed to be an alien assault on his body, the medical doctors concluded that nothing physical was wrong with Alexander and his girlfriend. Instead, he recommended psychological counseling. I suggested to Alexander that counseling is not necessarily such a bad idea. Anyone who has undergone such a traumatic experience should have someone more skilled than a UFO researcher helping him with his fears and subsequent paranoia. No matter how intriguing the case, the health of the individual is always the top priority.

> I took a small safety pin, sterilized it, and inserted it into three of the punctures. They were at least two centimeters deep and hit a nerve if forced.

I emphatically recommended that Alexander never perform such a dangerous investigation ever again, that his poking with the "sterilized" safety pin might result in nerve damage. This was the last I heard from him. I do not believe he liked my advice, which was rationally concerned for his well-being. I did let him know that I did not think he was crazy or delusional. I think Alexander wanted a more certain reply from me. But it was not my place to stoke his imagination concerning the abduction. I just wanted him to be medically and psychologically evaluated so he could heal from the trauma, instead of using his experiences, stringing him along, and squeezing paranoiac accounts from him. Frankly, he needed an individual trained in hypnotic regression, and that was way beyond my ability. For what it was worth I felt it important to record Alexander's experience. He would have to seek his own answers.

LAURA

I began shortly thereafter to correspond with Laura, another abductee, from Wisconsin. Laura has experienced multiple sightings of UFOs, missing time, alien abductions, radiation exposure tests and branding, illness and implants, as well as psychic and precognitive visions. She corresponded with me via email several times, tantalizing me with her mysterious experiences, which occurred between 2001 and 2014.

> So much has happened between 2001 and now. Strange occurrences did not begin until around the tragedy of 9/11, as if the giant cosmic pot was all stirred up. When the second Gulf War started, I was feeling so sad about how so many would suffer.
>
> I was driving my boss home from work at 9 p.m., heading north on Route 46. We drove right past the Cardinal Catholic retreat, 400 acres of woods set aside for the nuns and priests. Suddenly, I yelled to my boss and pointed at a hovering black triangle at about 500 feet, just above the trees and absolutely silent. I turned the car around as she screamed, "Get away from it!" She was terrified, but at least I had a witness.

Sightings of black triangular craft have become very common, from the Belgian wave to my best friend's encounter with a craft that flew low over his house, emitting a deep thrumming noise that rattled the windows. Laura's sighting must have been quite dramatic, with the craft above the trees and her boss screaming. But this sighting took place in a locale very dear to Laura, the "magic kingdom," a place to which she had returned for solace and peace.

> I was again in what I call the "magic kingdom," a place of impenetrable silence. Between 2:30 and 3:00 a.m., my shar pei Buddha dog, Nortie, signaled to me he had to go out. Everyone was fast asleep inside. It was foggy, and a thick mist surrounded me and Nortie, while two beams of light hung over our heads. The bright bluish-white beams were separated in two parallel lines of light that were horizontal in the sky, the top beam shorter than the bottom beam. I stood there amazed, confused, and then afraid. I went inside and tried to wake up all five people in the cabin, but nobody would listen to me and get up to see the lights. If someone tried to get

me up to see an unidentified object, I would go. Why did nobody get up? I still do not know.

As with other abduction reports, Laura was the only person (aside from her dog) to witness the strange horizontal light beams in the sky. Everyone else in the cabin seemed to be "switched off." Was Laura subsequently abducted during this experience? Hazarding a guess, I would have to say yes.

We have been visiting the "magic kingdom" for fourteen years now, and all the experiences I have had here have made me a little uneasy. Several strange incidents have occurred and my husband Doug has witnessed some of the physical evidence. I told my husband I did not want to come here this year. I had anxiety about it. I told my husband, they are coming back. It has been ten years since I saw the lights overhead in the middle of the night. My husband believes my experiences because he also has witnessed evidence that is strange and unexplainable. Despite my anxiety, we have come to this place again.

Now we are here and the pipes are busted. We are the first to open the A-frame every year, and obviously the closer did not drain the pipes correctly, so they froze in the winter. Doug went to town to get plumbing materials.

I went to lie on the large deck looking out over the lake at precisely 2:00 p.m., under clear skies and sunshine. The lake property is 700 acres, next to thousands of forested acres. I closed my eyes and felt an overwhelming peace and heard complete silence, a state of perfectly magical Zen. I noticed patterns above me like fractal geometry, with red and orange light.

Then I saw a very bright moving object. I opened my eyes to see if a tree was hanging over, thinking perhaps the leaves were swaying. But there was nothing above me. I heard two loud sounds next to me, as if something very large was scraping across the length of the deck. For some reason I did not even open my eyes to investigate the source of the sounds. I lay there unmoving for an hour. But it did not seem like an hour.

When Doug arrived with the plumbing parts, I said, "Boy, you got back fast!" He proceeded into the dark, dingy basement and asked for my help with the plumbing. I told him I was not feeling well and went to the bathroom. I took my pants down and noticed large patterns of very red triangular geometric shapes on my upper thighs. They were so bright red that they appeared to be burned into my skin. I was wearing jeans, so it could not have been sunburn. I had a lot of pain in my upper thighs and felt sick.

Here is the first direct evidence that Laura had been abducted and experimented upon, then returned to her deck chair. She noted missing time and what might have been induced paralysis. She apparently heard the Grays doing something near her that caused a loud scraping noise across the deck. Perhaps this was a piece of machinery the Grays brought with them. Maybe this abduction was a house call. Laura's "magic kingdom" is miles from any population center. Maybe the Grays felt secluded enough to conduct experiments on Laura at her cabin instead of on board their craft. Wherever the abduction experience occurred, Laura suffered from radiation exposure symptoms. She had triangular burns on her upper thighs and felt ill. Triangular patterns on abductees' bodies are quite common. I suspect that some of these patterns, especially the burns, are akin to a branding, marking the abductee as property. Later, Laura's husband, Doug, would hear the same loud scraping noise that she had heard prior to her abduction.

> Doug was under the deck when he suddenly screamed, "Laura! Did you hear that?" He said he heard something large scraping across the deck above him. I told him I had heard the same noise and I showed him the marks on my legs. He said, "What the heck is that?"
>
> That evening, my skin was peeling all over in small scales; even my eyelids were peeling. I used lotion to moisten the skin but nothing helped. It took a week for my skin to heal. I have been sunburned before, even had second degree burns from fishing on the boat with my dad in full sun, but I had never experienced this kind of flaking."

Even though Laura was covered up when she lay on the deck she received a large dose of radiation, enough to kill the outer layers of skin. The Grays apparently performed some kind of radiation experiment on Laura, probably with the large device she heard scraping along the deck. Any speculation as to why the aliens did this is beyond my reckoning. Whatever their reasons, they succeeded in burning Laura's body so badly that no conventional treatment seemed to help her condition, and she felt "sick," a common response to large doses of radiation exposure.

> Three days later, I felt something in my right ear. I freaked out and asked Doug to take a look. I thought that maybe a tick was in my ear. Doug looked and said he saw something, but he could not see it clearly. I felt behind my right ear and felt a nodule, a large protruding lump with a point at the end. I had weird sensations in my ear and headaches for several days. I could not touch it without a little discomfort. A week and a half later, I could touch it without pain.
>
> At this point, I began to wonder if I had been abducted.

Only at the moment when Laura found an apparent implant behind her right ear did she begin to entertain the awful possibility that she had been abducted. Perhaps the previous experiences had not been dramatic enough or what she would have consciously expected from an abduction encounter, but an implanted "nodule" that created "weird sensations in [the] ear and headaches for several days" was solid enough evidence of abduction for Laura to consider it seriously.

After a week of pain in her ear, the implant stopped hurting. The body must have required time to accept the foreign object.

> One night, I felt something tangled in my hair. It turned out to be a tick, and Doug removed it. But I also felt a scab on the right side of my scalp. It was long and narrow, directly above the nodule sticking out of the skin behind my ear.

Was the long and narrow scab the insertion area for the implant? This implantation was like shoddy surgery compared to most of the reported implant procedures. Did the Grays first make an incision in the outer ear prior to implantation? In any case, the implant caused Laura a lot of pain and anxiety. I received the following from Laura via email during a period of depression brought on by the abduction(s):

> I need to talk to someone with experience in the field of alien abduction. But I don't know who to trust. Nobody cares anyway. Now I am extremely depressed. What's the point? We all die anyway. After reading this you probably think I'm looney.

I immediately assured Laura that I did not by any means consider her to be "looney." At the same time, I was concerned for her physical and mental health. Again, risking loss of trust from the abductee, I highly recommended a check-up with a medical doctor and counseling as needed. I was not trained to help her with any of her experiences. All I could do was "listen" and record her amazing experiences. Laura was not a story. She was a confused person and a pained victim. Now she was experiencing depression and anxiety.

> I have been awaking with anxiety again. The other night I was on the deck at 3:30 a.m. At first, I heard no sound, only a creepy silence. Suddenly, I again heard the scraping sound on the deck, followed by a ringing noise. Terrified, I ran inside. I told my husband about the scraping and ringing noises. All was silent outside, so I ventured back out onto the deck. Everything was so quiet. Then I heard the strange noises again. The milkweed beyond the deck was glowing. Frightened yet again, I immediately ran back inside the cabin.

So the aliens had returned to the deck to perform procedures on Laura again. However, this time was different. Whatever that huge machine was that kept scraping across the deck, it was apparently some sort of medical device. This time, instead of radiation burns and implants, the Grays used the machine for something entirely novel and almost unheard of. Laura had been suffering from gall stones. She said that at one point during this procedure, she felt something healing. She saw a medical doctor not long after and discovered that the painful gall stones from which she had been suffering had completely disappeared! What could this healing possibly have to do with the aliens' experimentation? Could we but for a moment imagine this as a small act of mercy and goodwill, perhaps a reward for the other invasive and painful tests? I would tend to think not, but the evidence is here. For whatever reason, the Grays that had been abducting and experimenting on Laura had decided that they might as well heal her of this one affliction. Unless, of course, the gall stones held some unknown fascination for them, in which case we can forget about any benevolent intentions.

> Coming home from the city last night, at 11:00 p.m., the sky was dark with no moon. All of a sudden, my husband and I saw twenty or more lights glowing and floating in the sky above, to the right of the expressway. At first I thought they were high towers with lights. As we got closer they seemed lower, perhaps under radar, at about 1,500 feet in the sky. They produced no sound and appeared as glowing orbs! I screamed at my husband to pull over. I had my camera and wanted to take some shots of the orbs. But my husband refused to pull over and park. Other cars were slowing down to observe the orbs. My husband thought the orbs were some kind of advertising. All those glowing, hovering orbs were not advertising, especially at 11:00 p.m. on a Sunday! They were amazing! My husband insists they were Chinese sky candles floating way up high—but in the airspace of O'Hare International Airport? I am certain they were not sky candles, as they would represent a hazard to planes, and to cars on the expressway. I believe my husband is in denial that they were UFOs.

Laura's report of glowing orbs over the O'Hare International Airport is astonishing! Orbs are a mode of travel for the Grays, as reported by abductees. An orb can contain one or many Gray life forms. Chinese lanterns or some advertisement publicity stunt do not sound likely, especially considering the lights' proximity to O'Hare. But this sighting was not the beginning of the experience—it was the culmination of another!

> It occurred to me later that I had composed a painting called **INBOUND EXPRESSWAY ANGELS**, depicting floating orbs of light in the sky above the expressway. I think I may possess the extrasensory talent of precognition. I had composed another painting, just before 9/11, of two buildings falling on people.
>
> I recently had a terrifying dream that I was assaulted, and I have found a psychiatrist who is willing to perform hypnotic regression on me.

Laura had already seen the orbs over O'Hare—indeed, she had painted them as if she were being directed to do so by a higher intelligence, almost like composing an invitation to be fulfilled.

> I always wake up at the same time, 3:15 a.m. I heard someone calling my name repeatedly from another part of the house. Maybe I was dreaming. But it woke me up from a dream. Later that morning, I told my husband about my name being called. This has happened before, so he just thought my imagination was running wild again.

I noticed a lot of helicopters lately over the area. Later in the day, I saw a black helicopter circling around my subdivision. I could see it only two miles from my house. I got the feeling they were looking for something.

Black helicopters are seen quite often by abductees, perhaps in search or pursuit of the aliens, while simultaneously communicating the message: "We are watching you, too." Wherever the aliens are, the black-ops are not far behind. Maybe the Grays and the shadow government really are working together, as has been suggested repeatedly in ufology.

At 10:30 p.m., I saw a bright, very reddish, blinking light. I called my husband to come look. It was too big to be a planet or a star. We saw a plane coming towards us, just to the right of the blinking light. Then the plane just disappeared, but the blinking light remained. Then it moved to the north and shortly thereafter, it too disappeared. "I hope you don't disappear," my husband said, and that freaked me out.

I can only agree with Laura's husband, Doug. I, too, hope Laura does not disappear.

Several months passed since I had last heard from her. Then in January 2014, I received an email from Laura. She had not disappeared after all!

Spring, 2013. I got up suddenly out of a sound sleep with an anxiety attack. The cabin was absolutely silent. My son and his friend were sleeping upstairs in the loft. My husband was sleeping next to me. Nobody made a sound, not even snoring.

I walked to the tiny bathroom next to a window, grabbing my purse on the way. The toilet is maybe twelve inches from the window, which was open because it was hot this spring. The window shade was pulled down. I sat on the toilet and opened my purse. I took out a bottle of Xanax, the only cure for my panic attacks. When we left for this vacation, I had my prescription refilled, but had not counted or taken any as of yet. I closely examined the prescription bottle and realized the quantity appeared considerably shy of 100 pills. So I started to count. I poured all the pills into one hand and dropped one into the bottle. The pill dropping into the bottle was so loud! That was how quiet the cabin was—Zen. I spread the pills apart by tens and multiplied them.

Suddenly, I heard a loud, slow scratching noise on the window's heavy gauge screen. My heart felt like it literally stopped. I could not move. I felt as if my stomach was in my throat. I was actually paralyzed until I heard again the loud, slow scratching on the heavy gauge screen. I ran to the bed where my husband was sleeping and attempted to awaken him unsuccessfully.

The next morning I told the boys and my husband about the incident and they all laughed—until they went out to take a look at the screen. Two heavy, deep, diagonal scratches in the screen were undeniably real.

Only the day before, my husband had checked all the screens for holes because the mosquitoes were so abundant. Also, my son and his friend had stacked the garbage and recycled materials all over the porch, and right under the bathroom window screen, including two coolers. It was impossible to navigate through the garbage and recyclables on foot without making an awful lot of noise. So it seems to me whatever was trying to get my attention was...levitating!

Laura appears to have had another abduction experience. The cabin was silent. She was missing pills from her prescription bottle, perhaps an artifact of missing time or memory. Her husband was "switched off." Something, perhaps a Gray, had levitated over a deck covered in stacked garbage and recycling to frighten Laura by tearing into the window screen. Why? Again, the motives are inscrutable.

I present these two, now documented, cases of alien abduction as evidence that the Grays are abducting people in order to cause harm. Puncture wounds, bruises, and illness; radiation burns, sickness, and implants. I find nothing positive in these examples except that the abductees are presumably still alive, and this is reassuring. Is the information gathered by the Grays in these experiments actually relevant to their tests? I sincerely doubt it. I am more convinced that the aliens are actively torturing people and branding them as property. We are little more than lab mice, running the same mazes year after year. As long as They are here and so are we, alien abductions will continue. This is what the Grays do to people.

CHAPTER THREE

BORAX AND THE PILLOW BANDIT

Three unremarkable years went by before Earl Heriot had his next mysterious experience. It happened when he was in high school, on what was supposed to be a fun, carefree weekend. Earl and his best friend, Pete Marcusi, took an auto trip with Pete's father to visit his grandfather out in the California desert. Pete's grandpa lived alone in a ranch-style home located a short ride from the town of Boron, California. Boron is situated just north of Edwards Air Force Base, 125 miles northeast of Los Angeles, and on the western edge of the Mojave Desert. The world's largest open pit borax mine, U.S. Borax Boron Mine, operates there. The area is famous for its extensive borax deposits, with almost half of the world's refined borates coming from the mine.

Earl says this trip happened when he was in eleventh or twelfth grade. He thinks the year was 1965, because he remembers that he and Pete were talking about the new clad coins issued that year to replace silver dimes, quarters, and half-dollars.

> I knew something odd was going on before we even left Lakewood. Pete's dad was driving his small pickup while Pete and I sat in back in the camper. I was staring out the window as we made small talk, when suddenly it looked like bright green "liquid light" was running down the camper windows in thick rivulets, like water in a heavy rain. The green was so bright it glowed. While this was going on, I thought, "What the hell?" but I didn't say anything about it, and Pete didn't seem to see it, or at least he didn't mention it. It didn't last very long, maybe five minutes, but it freaked me out. I thought maybe I was going nuts. But what was odd is that otherwise, everything was normal. Neither of us did drugs or drank. We didn't even smoke cigarettes. We were pretty straight kids. A couple of nerds who got good grades and never got into trouble. So that green "liquid light" seemed to be a warning of the bizarre weekend that was ahead.

Earl says they met up with Pete's grandfather in Boron and he drove the boys out to his place in an old Jeep while Pete's dad took the pickup alone.

> His grandpa was this cool old desert rat. I liked him right away. A real salty character. He didn't have any neighbors for miles. Liked living alone out there. For fun he roamed the desert, collecting junk. One of the first places he took us to once we unpacked at the house was up to this remote area where there were ancient petroglyphs carved up on some rocks on a hill. The place had an eerie spiritual feeling to it. Later, back at his house, he showed us his garage that was full of boxes of stuff he'd picked up in the desert. Stone-age axes, projectile points, stone mortars and pestles, Native American relics. Lots of rusty junk from abandoned cars and machinery. Being typical teenagers, we thought it was all very cool.

That night, they sat around in the living room listening to Pete's grandfather tell stories about his life in the desert. Earl thought Pete's grandpa was a fascinating guy, a romantic figure, and maybe a role model for Pete and Earl. He dreamed that someday he could be like the old man, retired, with his own place, enjoying life far from the noise and chaos of civilization.

When it came time for bed, Pete and Earl rolled out their sleeping bags in the living room, with Pete's dad and grandpa each having a bedroom in the house. They were all tired after a long day and it should have been a quiet, restful night.

It wasn't.

He remembers standing outside the house in the cold, right before sunrise. It was still very dark, and the sun was just coming up in the east, breaking through the clouds in a dramatic way.

> It was like the light was making the evil darkness scatter and hide.

But Earl was absolutely terrified. He had the nagging feeling that something awful had happened the night before, in the utter pitch-black surrounding and engulfing the isolated desert home. All he had in his mind in the way of a clue as to what had transpired were two simple words that shattered any sense of security he might have felt up to that point in his life:

"They came."

He couldn't say who "they" were, or what had happened to him and the others in the house when "they" arrived. He does sense that, like the sun the next morning, "they" came from out of the east.

Pete appeared to be as disturbed as Earl was by the mysterious events in the night. But the two teenage boys didn't talk about it. They had a good breakfast, and got on with their weekend adventure.

Pete's grandpa let them ride an old motorcycle he had. He also gave them lessons in target shooting with a .22 caliber rifle, plinking at tin cans.

Earl remembers the area as having countless huge mounds of pink borax that had been dug from the earth, and that trucks raced back and forth constantly on the roads, carrying loads of the material. The boys gathered up specimens, and Earl came home with a shoebox full of pink crystals that he kept as a souvenir.

Other than one more odd thing that happened, the rest of the weekend was normal. They had a great time, although it was overshadowed by a heavy feeling of dread as each night approached.

He doesn't think "they" came again, although he's not certain of it.

The one additional odd thing was that on one occasion, Earl and Pete wandered far from the grandpa's house and onto what must have been Edwards Air Force Base territory. There was a sign warning them not to enter, but they did anyway. It was wide-open desert, with no improvements of any kind in sight, and they continued to walk until they realized they were lost, not knowing which direction it was back to the house. After another hour of wandering, they were very thirsty and the hot sun beating down on them didn't help the situation any.

"I could sure use a drink of water," Earl complained.

"No problem. There's plenty around here!" Pete said in his usual ironic manner. Of course, there wasn't any sign of water, or of any civilization.

It began to occur to the boys that they might be in trouble if they didn't find their way back soon.

And then, out of the blue, they saw a nonsensical sight up ahead. There was a water pipe coming up out of the desert, with a spigot on the end of it. The pipe rose about three feet from the desert floor. There were no other pipes, no irrigation equipment, no signs of human activity, for miles around. Just that one water pipe sticking up right where they needed it. It seemed like magic— like it had materialized there solely for their use. Earl turned the spigot and cold water gushed out. Both boys drank their fill, and when they were satisfied, they turned off the spigot and walked on. Soon they were back in an area they recognized, and shortly after that they returned safely to the grandfather's house.

Earl thought there was something almost supernatural about that water pipe being out there, all by itself, just when they needed water.

After the trip ended and he was back home in Lakewood, Earl realized it had been a very strange weekend, but he tried to put it out of his mind and didn't make any notes about the experience. That the trip actually happened is beyond doubt. His unease concerns the first night there and the two words, "They came." Who was it that so terrified him and Pete, and why couldn't he remember anything about "them" the next morning?

It's as if all memory of that night was erased from my mind. There's nothing left there in that time slot except for a lingering fear and the words, "They came." I'm not normally afraid of the dark. But the next morning, when we were waiting for the sun to come up, the blackness of the sky seemed like the most awful thing imaginable.

In his junior or senior year of high school, Earl Heriot had a strange out-of-body experience (OBE) that ended with a visit to a UFO. This happened unexpectedly one afternoon when he was in his bedroom in the Lakewood house (the room he shared with Rooster), goofing around with a jaw harp. This small musical instrument has a metal frame, which the player clutches between his teeth. A metal reed attached to the frame is plucked to make a musical note. The player's jaw acts as a resonator, amplifying the sound. Earl quickly noticed an unpleasant side effect of playing the harp; it created a strong vibration in his head.

"The thing was literally rattling my brain," Earl said with a laugh. Continuing, he said:

Well, that didn't feel very good and I was worried it might loosen the fillings in my teeth, so I decided to make an ad hoc adaptation to the instrument's design, to lessen the vibration. I don't remember exactly what I did but it involved knotting together several large rubber bands in a kind of daisy chain and attaching one end of that to the jaw harp. I think I attached the other end to a shoebox. My plan was that I would hold the jaw harp in my teeth as before, but this time I would pluck the rubber bands instead of the reed, and if I was lucky, the shoebox would act as the resonator instead of my skull. What I discovered is that my head still vibrated when I plucked the rubber bands, but at a much lower frequency. It was less jarring to me than when I played the harp the regular way, so I tinkered with it for a while, producing different notes by making the rubber bands tighter or looser.

And then a weird thing happened. It was no doubt brought on by that low frequency vibration affecting my brain, but I had a bizarre out-of-body experience. It wasn't like the OBEs I had as a kid, where I was peacefully floating up into the sky while I was asleep. In this experience, I instantly found myself seeing the world from the perspective of a very high altitude, like I was in space, orbiting the Earth. Even weirder, I seemed to be inside some mysterious alien craft. I didn't see any aliens, but instinct told me this was not "one of ours," as they say. I was up there, in that orbiting spacecraft or satellite, for ten or fifteen minutes. Apparently, I'd stopped plucking the rubber bands as soon as my consciousness left my body. When I came to and returned to normal, finding myself back in my bedroom, I discovered that during this altered state of consciousness, I'd gotten up from the bed where I'd been sitting, had fetched paper and pen, and had written something down. I guess you'd call it an example of "automatic writing," which I'd read about but had never experienced.

I was fascinated by Earl's uncanny experience and interrupted him to ask if he still had that document he'd written during the OBE.

I do. It's somewhere among my papers. I haven't looked at it in years, but my impression is that it was like a Surrealistic prose poem, full of strange images and expressions, but it didn't make a hell of a lot of sense.

"If you find it can I take a look?" I asked.

"Sure. No problem. I'm certain I kept it."

A week later, Earl loaned me the "automatic writing" document that he'd found in a file of miscellaneous writings labeled "Poems & Stories, 1967-1970." It's two and a half pages long, untitled and undated; however, a comment about a friend confirms it was written in high school.

Earl's present memory of the piece is fairly accurate, with the exception that—contrary to his claim that "it didn't make a hell of a lot of sense"—there is a clear underlying meaning once you filter out all the surreal images. As a whole, it can be described as a prose poem that conveys a metaphysical message. While parts are humorous, overall the tone is quite serious, and it has an air of emphatic certainty to it. There are no overt references to UFOs or aliens, but several lines do suggest that it was composed during an out-of-body experience, and that Earl was mentally visiting another dimension while he wrote. The following excerpt (with deleted passages replaced by three dots enclosed in brackets) reveals what Earl experienced during the minutes that his consciousness was separated from his physical body and allegedly aboard an orbiting craft:

The flight of matter through time and space, yes oh god now I know, yes I know. [...] Now I know there is no Hell / heaven I have been there / some say I am on a trip now / no, I am just visiting here / I am an independent traveler through this closet of toys [...] oh god how big everything is / I am spiritual now—you don't believe / it can't matter at all / I suppose all will know someday or am I special? This all doesn't exist in the other world (I am living on 2 planes / how to explain I won't and can't [...] there is always and forever / I don't remember my own History / why should I [...] believe me I fly / black sweet music / Glory there is no death or calendar [...] this body of mine is new to me / where I am from / silent laugh [...] supposedly to the old men in the "library" (for lack of a better term) I don't live in both [dimensions] / or at least to realize oneness at this stage is either an accident (oh hell!) or genius / I'm not smart [...] my world body is dumb as is the mind I have that lives here, or there depending on where I am / the clock has a million years in it / I must go, love you whatever, I don't care how I know / I say to myself please remember!!

The message buried in this rambling text reads like it's one part of his "being" that exists in a spiritual realm trying to communicate with another part of him: the part that lives in the normal, everyday world. Are the "old men in the library" some kind of spirit guides or mystical Elders? Earl says he doesn't know who they are, although he does have a mysterious memory of having once been in a large temple or classical-looking building where he was taught things by old men with long hair and beards and wearing robes. The building was similar to a museum, with row after row of glass-topped display cases. By merely looking down at the items on display, Earl would absorb an understanding of subjects they represented. In this way, he says he learned much about history, science, religion, and other topics, although he doesn't consciously recall most of what he learned there. Perhaps this knowledge is hidden deep in his subconscious.

Heriot seemed very uneasy when he handed me the rediscovered "automatic writing" document.

It really shocked me, what I wrote in here. I had expected it might mention a spacecraft or being in orbit, but that stuff about being in another dimension, and how there is no heaven or hell, and the "other" me communicating a message for the "earthly" me—it's all pretty freaking creepy. This is a perfect example of why I don't want to be hypnotized, why I don't want to explore the possibility that I've been abducted by aliens. There could be more creepy stuff like this, or even worse, and then I'd have to live with that, wondering what it means, if it's really true—all that. Why subject myself to it? I value my peace of mind too much to risk hypnosis.

Earl told me that years later when he read science fiction author Philip K. Dick's 1981 novel *VALIS*, it immediately reminded him of his own weird out-of-body experience in high school. In that novel, aliens from the star Sirius have installed an artificial satellite in orbit around the Earth. The VALIS ("Vast Active Living Intelligence System") satellite uses pink laser beams to transmit mental images and messages to humans below. Dick believed that in real life he was being fed information from a similar alien object. Earl says that if the VALIS satellite is real, perhaps he had unwittingly established contact with it in 1966.

It took a little convincing before Earl agreed to continue with our investigation of his unexplained memories. I promised him that if any one of the stories got too weird, we would back away from it and move on to something he felt less threatened by.

On the day that Earl's maternal grandfather died in 1967, his mother saw an owl perched on the roof of the house next door, staring through the window at her. It stayed there all day long, watching her, and thinking the owl's behavior was strange, his mother took a photo of it. Later, she received news from family back East that her father had died on that exact date.

Earl explains that:

> She believed the owl was either an omen of his death, or that it was his spirit, saying goodbye to her. I had forgotten about this event until Rooster recently mentioned it to me, at which time I clearly remembered it. I saw my mom's photo of the owl way back then.

Like Earl's odd memory of cows in the fog, this incident is evidence of the involvement of aliens in the family's affairs. Apparitions of unusual owls are a common screen memory in many UFO abduction cases.

As an English lit major in college, Earl Heriot wrote a lot of poetry and fiction. Most of it was semi-autobiographical in nature and dealt with the ins and outs of daily life for a college kid as seen through the kaleidoscope of the 1960s counterculture. However, there was one piece he wrote that always felt odd to him and seemed out of place among his other writings. He says it was based on a strange dream he had of an aerial ship and a short, white being who boarded it for the purpose of robbing him and the other passengers. The dream ship was "like an old fashioned wooden sailing ship with masts and rigging and sails, but it traveled through the sky instead of on the water." Earl describes the short, white entity in the dream as "puffy, with a head too big for its body, and with pale, off-white skin, like the color of a mushroom."

Because its size, shape, and color were similar to that of a pillow, and the fact that it came to him at night while he was asleep, Earl gave the being in the dream the name "Pillow Bandit." The poem, which is unpublished, is titled "Account of The Pillow Bandit." Earl shared his handwritten, seven-page manuscript with me. It's dated 1969, Earl's third year of attendance at California State College at Long Beach (later the school's name was changed to California State University at Long Beach).

In the poem, interestingly enough, the ship is made of metal, not wood. He describes it as "this gigantic steam-liner, bolted steel-plate, of rust and gray." The poem's plot revolves around the narrator's search for the ship's power source, an engine that he assumes must drive the vessel. He never finds it. The ship seems to be traveling outside the time/space continuum of physical reality. He writes, "we float, adrift, beyond time, beyond cause, to dream, asleep." He and the others on board look forward "with only anticipation to his feared arrival." In other words, they know this strange being, the Pillow Bandit, is coming and they dread his arrival. Their fear is so strong they are soon "falling into quarreling, panic struck, predicting each what he will do."

As he searches for the non-existent engine, the narrator finds himself "wondering who owns this ship…and how we came to be here."

In one of the marginal notes that are part of the poem, Earl writes in a Fortean manner, "Strange lights about the moon."

The ship passes through a weirdly lit, other-worldly environment. "The sky is strange out here, like a light against a silver screen, all is seen with photographic grain, thin and transparent, dull and unreal, and the light falls from no sun."

The poem's pace picks up as "a vessel to the north, sinister, approaches." This is the pirate ship, bearing the dreaded Pillow Bandit. Soon, "the vessel is spotted nearer, its Jolly Roger flying, the women wail and weep. Only minutes later, comes a fog from nowhere and hides our moans in pea soup."

The Pillow Bandit's appearance is bizarre and nonhuman. "The Pillow Bandit boarded to our horror, no legs, no arms, no face, a terrifying stuffed fat pillow with a gun belt strapped about [it]." As his accomplices relieve the passengers of their "rings, gold watches, jewels and billfolds," the Pillow Bandit "laughs with deep feathered voice." The poem ends with the passengers thanking God that he's gone but preparing for the Pillow Bandit's possible return.

I asked Earl if he realized just how much this weird prose poem sounded like an alien abduction account.

He did: "That's why I mentioned it in the first place when you asked about my strange memories."

Earl says he often has bizarre dreams and thinks nothing of them, but this one felt really different. "It meant something important, like it symbolized an experience my mind wasn't able to deal with directly. Or, that it was a suppressed memory leaking out of my subconscious in spite of the programming that was supposed to block it."

Shortly after he had the dream, Earl documented it in the poem, and as he wrote, further details emerged. It morphed from a dream about a wooden ship in the sky to the tale of a metallic craft traveling through an alternate dimension where humans—who had no idea how they had gotten there—trembled in fear at the pending arrival of a sinister being that very much resembled a partially blocked mental image of a Gray alien. An alien who is there to take something away from them.

One of Earl Heriot's closest friends in college was a psychology major named John Silver (pseudonym). John went by the nickname "Long John Silver," the pirate in Robert Louis Stevenson's novel Treasure Island. Unlike Earl, who in the '60s was a so-called "weekend hippie" who wore his hair long but bathed daily, got good grades and worked steadily, John was a card carrying, dyed-in-the-wool hippie. Most days, Silver was stoned on LSD, peyote, magic mushrooms, hashish, or some other psychedelic substance. He practically chain-smoked marijuana. Earl smoked pot only occasionally, more as a social thing than to get high, and he swears he never tried anything stronger.

Many people Heriot's age were experimenting with LSD during the sixties. According to Heriot:

LSD scared the crap out of me. I valued my sanity far too much to try that stuff. I'd heard stories about people who dropped acid once and ended up in a mental ward. Pot, on the other hand, didn't worry me. It had the same effect on me as a couple of beers. In those days, the marijuana you could buy all over the place was cheap, pure, and mild. It wouldn't make you hallucinate. I never even had any weird fantasies while smoking grass. It simply relaxed me, made me mellow. In fact, the only odd, UFO-type experiences I had during my later years in college—which is the only time in my life during which I smoked grass—were all related to John Silver in some way, and those were always at times when I had not recently smoked pot and was not under its influence. I don't attribute these unusual events or thoughts to the effects of having pot in my system; I attribute them to John himself. He was a freaky character.

Earl tells me that it was during these later college years, approximately 1968 to 1973, that he began collecting books about UFOs. He says:

Well, when John Silver found out about my UFO book collection, he got intensely interested in the subject and started his own collection. As much as he was a lazy, hippie bum—and I say that with affection—John had a strong competitive streak in him and it wasn't long before he was trying to out-do me, to find more books, better books, rarer books than I had. I went with him to this antique shop in Long Beach where the owner had a complete run of the old 1950s Ray Palmer-edited pulp magazine, FLYING SAUCERS (originally titled FLYING SAUCERS FROM OTHER WORLDS), starting with the very first issue. John bought the entire run of magazines for $40, which was a lot of money in those days and it left him with no food money for the rest of the month. That's how John was—a balls-out kind of guy. As John's book collection grew, it took over major portions of his crummy little apartment. I came over one day and he showed me how the kitchen cabinets were completely packed with contactee books from the 1950s and '60s, with no room left on the shelves for even a box of Wheaties™ or can of beans.

Once it was clear that his collection had mine beat, John tried to take things to the next level. He begged me to sell him all my UFO books. I didn't want to part with them, but he was relentless, nagging me endlessly, and I finally gave in and sold my books to him. I don't remember for how much. Then he had both my collection and his. Good for him. I didn't really care. I just started buying other copies from the used bookstores in town, and didn't tell him I was rebuilding my collection.

The competition for vintage flying saucer books was just the start of John and Earl's joint involvement in the subject of aliens. On two separate occasions, Earl and his wife Jane (pseudonym) took trips by car with John Silver from Long Beach to locations out in the California desert. Earl says he remembers almost nothing about these trips—which were brief visits of a few hours' length made during daylight hours—except that on both occasions, John had talked excitedly beforehand about finding alien bases and UFO landing sites, meeting with aliens, and similar topics.

You would think I would recall that sort of thing, as sensational as it sounds, but when I search my mind, those trips are almost a complete blank. I have one very short memory of arriving at a remote desert location, parking the car by some large boulders, and then the three of us walking down a bare dirt slope toward a desolate-looking valley. That's from one of the trips. As for the other trip, I recall absolutely nothing. I think one of the locations was Joshua Tree National Park. It's about 140 miles from Long Beach. I have no idea what the other place was.

With anybody else, you would just assume they were kidding if they talked about contacting aliens, but not John. He seldom joked about anything, except maybe about how many times he'd taken LSD. He was a very intense guy, and he was utterly obsessed with the whole alien thing at that time. I think he really intended to make contact with something out there. Jane and I were just going along for the ride. I didn't have any burning desire to meet space beings. Reading about them was enough excitement for me.

Earl says he's always suspected something very unusual may have happened out there in the Southern California desert—if only he could remember it.

The only content I have in my mind when I think about that one visit that I recall a small part of is the idea that alien gods live there and we might have met them.

Earl does retain one definite visual impression relating to aliens and John Silver, but it's not set in a desert locale:

I remember standing inside the entrance to his cold, little apartment in Long Beach, like I'd just come in the front door and shut it behind me. In the middle of the dining room there's a high metal platform, sort of like a hospital bed. It's about belly button high on me, so it's taller than a normal bed. John is laid out on it and he's surrounded by several tall insect-like beings. They're quite a bit taller than me, and I'm six foot, so they're maybe seven feet tall. There are about half a dozen of them. They look a lot like insects with bug eyes, large heads, and spindly bodies. Their hands are coming in at him. Not exactly like the tall praying mantis critter I saw in junior high school. These are shorter and lighter in color.

A tan-gray tone. The beings are busy doing something to John and they ignore me.

I asked Earl if he's still in touch with John Silver, hoping I could interview Silver about the insectoid aliens, their trips to the desert, as well as any other UFO-related experiences he may have had, with or without Heriot. Unfortunately, Earl and Jane lost touch with Silver after graduating from college, and his present whereabouts are unknown.

Earl relates:

It ended badly with John. He developed this romantic crush on Jane and I grew more and more uncomfortable with having him around. A buddy of mine named Sal (pseudonym) heard about this situation and became very concerned. I filled Sal in on everything that had happened up until then, and Sal said he thought Silver was possessed by an evil spirit of some kind. Sal suggested I have a friend of his perform "an exorcism" to rid myself and Jane of John Silver's malign influence. Sal lived in a commune of sorts with a bunch of Jesus hippies and this exorcist fellow was one of the guys from the house they all shared. It was like something out of a bad horror film. The exorcist guy came over with Sal one night. The three of us sat around a small table in my apartment. Jane was working that night and wasn't home, which was good because I don't think she would have appreciated our "exorcism" of John, who she liked. I showed the exorcist a small snapshot of John Silver. "No doubt about it," the guy said. "I can see it in his eyes." The exorcist lit a candle, waved John's photograph over it while saying some prayers, and then touched the picture to the flame and set it on fire. He dropped the burning photo on a plate and let it turn to ash. "You're free of him now," the exorcist said, and we were. After that, I saw very little of John Silver and eventually lost all track of him when Jane and I moved to Oregon in 1973 after finishing school.

John was possessed by evil—no doubt about it. The question is, "Which evil?" And I think we all know the answer to that.

CHAPTER FOUR

PORTRAIT OF THE ARTIST IN GRAY

A rtistic expression is a useful tool for understanding the alien abduction experience and the aliens themselves. For the Grays, the artist is a form of communication technology, allowing the aliens to translate their psychic impressions into visual representations. An abductee may gain knowledge from his or her artwork that is either inspired or directed by the Grays. The relationship between artist and alien is discussed in this chapter with the work of Betty Andreasson, Budd Hopkins, David Huggins, and focusing on "Mr. Krister."

> MY PAINTINGS AND SCULPTURES, AT FIRST GLANCE, MAY APPEAR TO BE PURELY AESTHETIC; CLOSER UP, THEY ARE NOT. THEY HOLD A FEELING OF TENTATIVENESS, COMBINED WITH A SENSE OF ARRIVAL.
>
> —BUDD HOPKINS
> (1931-2011)

BETTY ANDREASSON

Betty Andreasson's abduction experiences, chronicled by Raymond Fowler in *The Andreasson Affair*, *The Andreasson Affair: Phase Two*, *The Watchers*, *The Watchers II*, and *The Andreasson Legacy*, have given ufology a very detailed look at the Grays and their technology. Raymond Fowler even refers to Betty Andreasson as "the aliens' living audio visual to mankind" in *The Watchers*.

Betty reported orbs (or "spheres" and "balls") several times during her hypnotic regression sessions. Fowler notes this as one of the Grays' paranormal abilities: "[The Grays can] transform their bodies into balls of energy and back again."

Betty's greatest contribution to ufology is the phenomenal amount of illustrations she produced in conjunction with hypnotic regression for the series of Andreasson books. Interestingly, much of the alien tech she sketches in amazing detail seems tailor-made to the human body, as if the craft were designed to transport human subjects. Indeed, they must have been, as their primary function is apparently a human-abduction laboratory.

On one trip with her Gray guides, Betty saw an actual phoenix, as if human mythology were coming alive for her. She also experienced strong religious experiences among the Grays. Journeying in another realm with the Grays, she was brought before a giant doorway that stretched to infinity. Beyond, said the aliens, was "the One." Though Betty was allowed to see "the One," she was unable to report to the researchers what she saw beyond the doorway. Her face was radiant and filled with joy, but she told the researchers repeatedly that she could not describe, and was not allowed, to tell anyone about "the One." Through Betty's eyes, "the One" was probably her vision of God.

BUDD HOPKINS

Ufology's own late great artist and alien abduction researcher, Budd Hopkins, produced abstract paintings, some of which are extremely similar to Mr. Krister's work (discussed in detail below). You can see what appear to be yellow egg-shaped orbs in his oil on canvas *Aphrodite's Garden* (1956), years before he saw a UFO (in 1964) or ever hypnotically regressed his first alien abductee. Other works incorporate bold shapes, like triangles and circles (e.g. *Marathon*, oil on canvas, 1964) as well as rectangles (e.g. *Jutland III*, serigraph, 1979). Other paintings appear to be abstract landscapes, again similar to Mr. Krister's work (e.g. *Study for August*, oil on Masonite, 1958, and *Green November*, oil on canvas, 1963).

The fact that Hopkins was both an accomplished artist and foremost researcher into alien abductions can be no accident. His sensitive mind appears to have been open to alien imagery in a very similar fashion to Mr. Krister, whether he realized this or not. Hopkins admits in *Art, Life and UFOs* that his 1964 sighting of a silver metallic disk did indeed affect his work:

Artists usually don't like to admit they're influenced either by other artists or by outside events, and for years I insisted that the 1964 UFO sighting had no lasting effect on my work. And yet, admit or not, we always know that many things can cause changes in our imagery...I can see that virtually everything I painted for the next twenty years contained a large, dominating circle of some sort...

This change in artistic expression began with *Sun Black I*, oil on canvas, 1966. How much Hopkins' art affected his ufology is a fascinating question with no answer now that Hopkins has passed on.

DAVID HUGGINS

The astonishing abduction artwork of David Huggins portrays a lifetime of contact with aliens in the book *Love in an Alien Purgatory: The Life and Fantastic Art of David Huggins*, written by Farah Yurdozu.

As a young boy Huggins was first introduced to a female hybrid, whom he called Crescent. Crescent took Huggins' virginity from him at the age of seventeen (*The First Experience*). She continued to engage in sexual intercourse with him throughout his life, producing dozens of hybrid children (*In My Room*, *Kissing*, and *Falling in Love*). Later, he was made to have intercourse with two other female hybrids (*Body Language*, *Show Us*, *Privacy*, and *We Are Waiting for You*).

Intriguingly, like Betty Andreasson, Huggins witnessed an actual phoenix from mythology, transforming from large bird to flames and finally to ashes and a large dark worm (*Phoenix, Flames,* and *The Worm*). Also, like Betty, Huggins was given a book by one of the small Grays, but was not allowed to keep it; all he remembers from the book is a circle with a cross inside (*Gray Alien Gives a Book* and *The Symbol*).

Huggins also saw many hybrid babies (*Baby In The Tube*, *Your Baby Is Dying*, *Touching the Baby*, *Visiting the Nursery*, and *Here's Your Baby*) as well as his own hybrid son, who appears to have been about ten years old (*Your Hybrid Son*). Many other paintings depict small Grays in blue suits, Mantis aliens, glowing saucer-shaped craft, and even a small furry biped. Huggins also painted alien-like landscapes, such as *Underground Caves*, depicting flying saucers parked in the nooks of a giant cave wall. Ultimately, David Huggins came to believe that "[the Grays] wanted him to do paintings about his experiences with them," again, much like Betty Andreasson acting as "the aliens' living audio visual to mankind."

MR. KRISTER

A notable example of the "artist as communication technology" is a local forty-three-year-old artist from Salem, Oregon, herein known as "Mr. Krister."

Many of his oil paintings include luminous human bodies and lots of glowing orbs. These orbs are obviously life forms, and in some paintings, the orbs are transforming into luminous bodies. Alien abductee accounts of bright orbs preceding an abduction are very common in ufology, and at least one example recounts the transformation of a glowing orb into a Gray. Other accounts mention the presence of multiple life forms inhabiting a single orb. In both cases, the orb is some form of living energy. Evidence suggests that this is one mode by which Grays can travel in space and time.

Mr. Krister's artistic vision, which has captured a fully detailed abduction experience, Gray faces and hybrid faces, "shadow people," and luminous orbs, clearly represents some form of alien contact. Whether these visions come from repressed memories of alien abduction (Close Encounters of the Fourth Kind) or psychic contact with aliens (Close Encounters of the Fifth or Eighth Kind— see Glossary), Mr. Krister is obviously channeling some form of alien communication. The precise nature of this contact is explored in the interviews that follow.

JORDAN HOFER (JH): Can you tell me about your Gray drawings?
MR. KRISTER (MK): I believed in aliens back in high school. For seven years I was fascinated by aliens. I don't remember why. The Grays were on a pedestal for me. I really believed they were real and that they had evolved technology a million years before humanity. Just think if we had another million years of technological evolution. One million more years of thinking. Maybe they are insane. Either way, they're here.

JH: Why do you think the Grays are insane?
MK: They rely on knowledge, the brain blabbering, on thinking too much. Even the good Grays are insane.

JH: Do you have any indication of what the Grays want and why they are here?
MK: They want to domesticate the human species. That's what the hybrids are about.

JH: Tell me about your hybrid drawings.
MK: I have had visions. I saw different faces when I looked in the mirror. I even looked like a hybrid alien back in my twenties. One of my graphites depicts an alien "cherub" wearing a mask.

JH: What is under the mask of the alien cherub?
MK: A hybrid Gray-human.

JH: What do you think of the hybrids?
MK: I used to believe the hybrids were our salvation. They will definitely replace us, as human beings. They are more like babies, more socially altered than the Grays.

JH: The idea of hybrids replacing humans does not sound like salvation. What are your thoughts on that now?

MK: It's because we're going extinct at a massive rate. The Grays will take the planet after we destroy ourselves. The Earth will be theirs alone, or else the Reptilians'.

The contrast between Mr. Krister's opinion of hybrids and the Grays who engineered them is striking. Whereas the Grays are insane from too many millions of years of "brain blabbering" knowledge, the hybrids are "cherubs," naïve, childlike, and hopeful. Some abductee reports of hybrids confirm this. Hybrids have been described at times as gentle, loving, sexually aware and adept, and also (especially the males) as socially retarded, empathetically challenged, and too sexually aggressive. In either case, at some point in their development, hybrids require humans to train them how to form healthy pair bonds and how properly to initiate sexual contact. The Grays have nothing to do with this training except for supplying their hybrids with human subjects.

While interviewing Mr. Krister, I found myself asking what are his dreams? Most of Mr. Krister's paintings could be described as "dreamscapes." I was interested in finding a connection between his alien art and his dreams, and whether he suspected any abduction experiences.

JH: Have you ever dreamed of aliens?

MK: I had a dream in high school in which I saw a Reptilian dressed in shiny, opalescent clothing. It carried a wood staff that encased a sphere of light with a weapon concealed inside. I saw three Grays. I remember levitating above them as they were looking at me. Then the Reptilian looked at me, and that's all that I remember. I thought it was real at the time.

JH: Do you suspect you were abducted?

MK: No, I only had that one dream. I floated out a window and to two trees out front my house. I watched the Reptilian and the Grays from there. I woke up from the dream in my bed.

JH: Can you tell me more about the Reptilian?

MK: It didn't look like the Gorn [from *STAR TREK*™]. Its eyes were smaller than Gray eyes. The Reptilian was in command and it was using the Grays as inferior life forms.

This dream with its Reptilian commander also coincides with some abductee reports. Reptilians are invariably described as more aggressive than the Grays. They seem to be in charge when Grays are also present. This suggests an interesting alien hierarchy and possible collusion. Do the Reptilians keep Grays as slaves and then use them to abduct us and perform experiments? Most probably, the Reptilians and Grays are not allies. The more aggressive Reptilians could be a superior competing species, using abducted Grays, or else the Reptilians themselves are merely Grays in the upper echelons of their hierarchy, presenting themselves as reptile screen images, playing in to old evolutionary memories of snakes (an ancient fear shared by both humans and chimpanzees, as well as vervet monkeys).

As noted prior, orbs are nearly ubiquitous in Mr. Krister's alien landscape art. They populate the landscapes like luminous wildlife. Orbs have been very common in ufology for decades, whether seen as UFOs or witnessed as glowing entities preceding an abduction. Most of them are about the size of a soccer ball, but they have been reported as small as a marble and as large as a car as well. Like all life forms, they display variation.

JH: What are the orbs in your paintings?

MK: They have the life force in them. Orbs are alive, just like Foo Fighters. I used to believe they were angels.

JH: What do you think they are now?

MK: They are animals like us. They use their technology to make them seem more than they are. I don't think they are pure vivacious energy. The bright light of the orb is a force field. They have antigravity technology. The orbs are Grays.

JH: Why do you create so many illustrations of orbs?

MK: They are the perfect shape. Orbs are easier to paint than trees.

Certainly the impetus to paint so many orbs goes beyond the simple fact that they are "easier to paint than trees," as true as that may be! The sheer preponderance of orbs in Mr. Krister's work over the past two decades suggests that a deeply ingrained vision is repeatedly forcing itself to the surface of his thoughts and onto his many canvases. In other words, if Mr. Krister painted primarily sea turtles, it would be obvious to the observer that the artist held some form of emotional and/or intellectual interest in sea turtles. The orbs are most probably arising from his subconscious; but why orbs, specifically? The alien contact and communication speculation seems the simplest answer to this question.

I wondered whether or not Mr. Krister had experienced any other forms of paranormal phenomena, usually classified outside the domain of UFOs and alien abductions.

JH: Have you ever had an out-of-body experience (OBE)?

MK: I suspect that I have had many OBEs, but I only remember one. I found myself on the ceiling. A silver cord was attached to my belly button. I was in the astral plane when I saw two small Grays staring at me.

OBEs and near-death experiences (NDEs) have been linked to UFO and alien abduction phenomena, so the fact that Mr. Krister once experienced an OBE, in the presence of Gray aliens no less, proves that his experience at the time was linked directly to alien communication. Lucid dreaming is also associated with alien contact, especially since dreams appear to be a hunting ground for the Grays.

JH: Tell me about your lucid dreaming experiences.

MK: I was manipulated in the dreams. The more aliens there were around me, the more malevolence I felt. I had bruises on my toe after a lucid dream.

This is an odd response concerning a lucid dream, since the dreamer is the one who gains the ability to control the dream. But in this case, under alien influence, the opposite seems to have occurred: the Grays were the dreamers and Mr. Krister was the dream! He was not in control of the aliens' actions or his response to them, but was subjected to feelings of "malevolence" and even physical trace markings as bruises on his toe!

Some of Mr. Krister's most compelling paintings are bizarre alien landscapes, many of them deserts with ominous skies, populated either by orbs or luminous idealized human and animal forms. Sometimes portals are visible, entering into strange new worlds. Orbs often emerge from or enter them. After viewing his many landscape paintings, the observer must ask whether these are simply dreamscapes or else psychic snapshots from alien worlds.

JH: Many of your landscapes are reminiscent of alien worlds. Could some of them be visions of another planet?

MK: Of course. The landscapes are empathetic visions seen through real eyes in other worlds.

JH: Do you believe you may be communicating with aliens?

MK: The aliens communicate through me onto canvas. I see nebulous and strange skies and they have to get that out of me. The aliens might be experimenting on my brain to see what happens when they make me paint.

JH: Do you believe you are receiving images from many aliens on many worlds, or just the Grays on different planets?

MK: I have seen Reptilians and Grays. I've only seen those two species and they're at war. Far away battles are fought by Reptilians and Grays. They each have physicians, scientists, warriors. Some of them are ethical, but they are in the extreme minority. Their wars are intergalactic.

JH: Okay, that's two species. Do you suspect others you have not been able to identify?

MK: Another was a Gray that looked human with dark, almost black, hair. Her large dark eyes were glowing. I was very calm. She wanted me to impregnate her.

Apparently, Mr. Krister experienced the same reproduction experiment as David Huggins, and engaged in sexual intercourse with a tall Gray wearing a wig, glasses, and human clothing!

MK: I made a small graphite drawing of the female Gray alien I call "Sara." She is wearing a short, black wig, horn-rimmed glasses, and a string strap tee shirt. I really think she is adorable, kind of the hot librarian type. This picture was familiar to me the moment I sketched it. She must have told me her name was Sara. Really, for all the bad things I think about the Grays, I honestly can't feel that way about Sara. I think I love her. She's tricking me but I don't care.

Mr. Krister sees and paints what the Grays want him to see and paint. The Grays are communicating with the observer in each of his alien landscape paintings, orb paintings, and drawings of Grays and hybrids. His art is the technology through which they communicate with him and the rest of us. He has no need of a radio telescope, like SETI! If this is true, just what are the Grays trying to communicate?

MK: Transcendence, and that could mean death.
JH: Is that a Gray threat?

MK: No, it is an observation they are making. We either wake up as a single organism or we go extinct, and then the Grays take over.
JH: Why do you think they are communicating these observations?

MK: They are sadistic. Like Whitley Strieber's abductions. The Grays are insane. They are waiting for us to kill ourselves off, and getting high on our suffering because they believe we are a stupid race.
JH: Are we a stupid race? Do you believe the Grays?

MK: Look where we're at. The oceans are dying. It may be the end of *HOMO SAPIENS*.
JH: You mentioned transcendence. Is that still an option?

MK: Transcendence and death are the same thing. Go to the mystics like the Buddha. There is hope.

Mr. Krister again returns to the belief that the Grays are insane and sadistic. They could rescue us from extinction, but they do not consider us worthy of being saved. The only hope, he says, comes from human mysticism. Ironic, then, that the uninformed may consider ufology a religion of belief instead of a tool of inquiry. But what did Mr. Krister think? Were some of his artistic images religious?

MK: Many of them are spiritual and religious in a pure sense. They have a benevolence about them. People like the paintings, especially teens.
JH: Are these spiritual and religious paintings iconic?

MK: I learned from iconic artists. Certainly the picture I did of crucified Grays is iconic. Now I communicate more specifically.
JH: Do you think the Grays want us to believe that contact and abduction are religious experiences?

MK: I wanted to be abducted for seven years. It was a religious hope.

I wondered if Mr. Krister ever felt like a "chosen one" to communicate for the aliens through his art, because the question is a mystery: "Why is Mr. Krister and not someone else illustrating these alien images?"

MK: There are not many orb artists. I am not an orb artist.
JH: What kind of artist do you consider yourself?

MK: I like painting, seeing new perspectives. Every painting I make is a learning experience. I also need to sell my art.
JH: So are you a kind of working artist?

MK: Yes. I sometimes paint by commission.
JH: Do you ever feel like the "chosen one"?

MK: If I believed that, I would believe in a lie. I feel pretty damn lucky, though. Maybe I *AM* the chosen one! (Laughter)
JH: Do you think you might be more naturally sensitive to psychic communication than most people?

MK: I'm sensitive, but I don't know if I'm psychic. Sometimes I see future events. I dream that Earth will not belong to the great apes in the future. But I have real, positive hope, a love that lies especially within the human heart.

I was excited to discover that Mr. Krister had already produced works of art as if in anticipation of my next line of questioning.

JH: Tell me about these three new pictures you have done.
MK: I keep seeing this giant black pyramid on the Grays' home planet. The first drawing in colored pencil shows the building far off beyond the landscape, casting shadows to the foreground from two suns behind it. There is a crater encrusted in golden glowing sulfur crystals—it leads to the underground dwellings where Grays used to live before they colonized the surface. Parts of the giant black building are eroding away. A Gray reconnaissance craft is in the foreground with a blue orb emerging from it to scan the surface. This is a vision from the Grays' post-apocalyptic planet.

The second vision I painted with ultraviolet. This time I'm looking up at the building from far below and I can see it stretching way up, with the suns on either side. A blue orb is rising up, either checking out the building or proceeding to enter it. I'm not sure if this is a vision from before the Grays' environmental apocalypse or not.

The third drawing I did with graphite and colored pencil. This time I am at the very top of the building, at the apex. And this is definitely before the Grays' planet was left barren. Amazingly, there is a gigantic city crowning the building's apex. It's huge—like bigger than London. There are two inflatable bags emerging from the structure below the city that look like giant weather balloons. I don't know what they are.

Mr. Krister's artwork of the giant black pyramid was a direct hit. He was seeing this object repeatedly and was compelled to portray it from different angles in space and in time. He even considered constructing a scale model of the massive structure that would have dominated his limited living space.

Before proceeding along the primary line of inquiry, I felt another approach might reveal more of Mr. Krister's subconscious awareness of a constant alien presence. I chose twenty words I felt best represented the abduction experience, but without cues for specific replies. The results of the free association word pairs are below:

JH: Night.
MK: Day.

JH: Bed.
MK: Fear.

JH: Window.
MK: Portal.

JH: Dream.
MK: Reality.

JH: Light.
MK: Floating.

JH: Darkness.
MK: Hope.

JH: Owl.
MK: Master.

JH: Ball.
MK: Glowing.

JH: Stars.
MK: Moving.

JH: Earth.
MK: Dead.

JH: Sky.
MK: Black.

JH: Eyes.
MK: Deep.

JH: Table.
MK: Laser.

JH: Mirror.
MK: Horror.

JH: Needle.
MK: Dirty.

JH: Sleep.

MK: Terrifying.

JH: Apartment.

MK: Haunted.

JH: Insect.

MK: Praying Mantis.

JH: Reptile.

MK: *GOJIRA* [Japanese title of original *GODZILLA* film].

JH: Love.

MK: Everywhere.

A brief analysis of the free association word pairs follows. Nearly all of the responses matched descriptions of alien abductions, suggesting that Mr. Krister has been abducted, whether he consciously remembers the experiences or not.

Night and Day are opposites, so the response of Day to Night is not surprising; it could, however, refer to the bright light of the UFO that often precedes abduction in the dark of night.

Bed and Fear, Window and Portal, Dream and Reality, and Light and Floating all describe alien abduction.

Darkness and Hope represents Mr. Krister's optimism despite this planet's environmental collapse.

Owl and Master is very interesting, suggesting the owl is a screen image of a Gray.

Ball and Glowing refers to the ubiquitous orbs.

Stars and Moving might be the memory of traveling through space on board a Gray craft.

Earth and Dead again refers to Mr. Krister's anxiety concerning the world's dying biosphere.

Sky and Black refers to space, perhaps a buried memory like the previous association Stars and Moving.

Eyes and Deep is an obvious description of the eyes of the Grays.

Table and Laser, Mirror and Horror, and Needle and Dirty all describe medical equipment used during alien abductions.

Sleep and Terrifying and Apartment and Haunted tell the when and where of Mr. Krister's more recent abductions.

Insect and Praying Mantis appears to be a memory of the Mantids.

Reptile merely reminded Mr. Krister of one of his favorite films, the original Godzilla movie, *Gojira*.

His final pair, Love and Everywhere, reflects Mr. Krister's unshakable optimism for the human heart.

The next logical phase of my investigation into Mr. Krister's art was to commission him to paint a landscape of the Grays' home planet! This would be a useful tool for comparative studies of other artistic alien landscapes, including his own works. I was also anxious to compare his painting with information I had read about the Grays' planet of origin in abduction reports.

JH: Are you familiar with any information concerning the Grays' home planet?

MK: No. I never looked into that. Just what I've painted and drawn, wherever that came from.

JH: Please answer the following questions as if you are painting their planet right now. What color is the alien sky?

MK: A reddish hue with some amber.

JH: Do you see any vegetation?

MK: I see strange flowers with glowing orbs on them.

JH: What does the air smell like?

MK: Vanilla, cinnamon, and sand, and a completely new smell.

JH: What is the temperature?

MK: There is one giant desert that spans one-third of the planet. In the day, temperatures rise to 900° Fahrenheit.

JH: Do you see any buildings or structures?

MK: Red glowing rectangles, squares, cubes, and hexagonal tunnels, cities carved out of rock.

JH: Do you see any life forms in the cities?

MK: Yes. Feathered mammalian scavengers with six eyes, like alien raccoons. They are the largest population of all life forms on the surface.

JH: Do you see any Grays?

MK: No, they're all gone. They're all extinct here. The ones that stayed, died.

Mr. Krister worked on the commissioned painting of the Grays' home planet, an oil on canvas, *Fragrance 9*, that took a total of ten hours' work. Immediately, I noticed the striking contrast between the realized painting and Mr. Krister's previous description of the alien planet. This was a snapshot from before the Grays' planetary apocalypse. His previous description of the planet was from a time after it became uninhabitable.

JH: FRAGRANCE 9 is a lot different than the planet you described before.

MK: FRAGRANCE 9 depicts life on the Grays' home planet before the apocalypse.

JH: Can you explain the details for me?

MK: The ground is alive with trillions of microscopic furry caterpillars. The female Gray is phasing from one reality to another—you can see through her. The blue orb to her right contains two of her mature clones. The Gray and the orb are looking at you. They are obsessed with you.

JH: Obsessed with the viewer of the painting?

MK: Yes. They are looking directly at you when you look at the painting.

A Gray phases in the alien landscape of *Fragrance 9. Oil on canvas, 24" x 18", by Mr. Krister, 2013. Photograph by Mark Madland, 2014.*

JH: Were you aware of a Gray presence while painting *FRAGRANCE 9?*

MK: Yes, I felt a lot of fear. As I painted, I thought I heard shuffling noises behind me. The Grays were watching me for a while.

JH: Thank you for the painting.

MK: I have no problem giving away this painting.

Later, Mr. Krister painted *Eye*, "A detail," he said, "of the alien in *Fragrance 9*—the better to see you with." Three small canvases glued one on top the other provide *Eye* a multi-dimensional space, like the female Gray phasing in *Fragrance 9*. And there is definitely a presence looking through the composition of *Eye*. I avoid looking into it for fear of it looking back—and it's always watching, even when the book is closed, its stare penetrates the pages and cover.

I commissioned Mr. Krister to paint *Fragrance 9*, but *Eye* was a "gift" I wish he had never opened for me.

From the case of Mr. Krister and the other artists profiled in this chapter, we can see how aliens use artists to communicate their visions, their memories, perhaps even their intentions. Of course, graphic artists are not the only group to act as "Gray-human communication technology." I experienced what I believe to be Gray meddling in the writing of my previous book, *Evolutionary Ufology*, and again here. Why is Mr. Krister among those apparently chosen to communicate for the aliens? I can only assume that his interest in aliens earlier in his life somehow attracted them to him, and led them to direct his art to their specifications.

The multi-dimensional *Eye* of the Gray alien in *Fragrance 9. Oil on three canvases, 3" x 3"*
with 3" x 2" and 2" x 2", by Mr. Krister, 2014. Photograph by Mark Madland, 2014.

It is impossible to conclude that this form of alien-directed communication is anything new to the human species. Betty Andreasson, Budd Hopkins, David Huggins, and Mr. Krister stand at the forefront of a communication technology with origins back tens of thousands of years to the earliest human practitioners of art and religion, the shamans who entered caves and emerged with power and knowledge.

CHAPTER FIVE

ENORMOUS FLAMING THING IN THE SKY

n January of 1973, Earl and Jane Heriot moved to Oregon and temporarily lived with Jane's parents on a farm just outside the city of Dallas while Earl looked for work. They stayed there until Earl found a job in nearby Salem, the state capital, at which time they moved to that larger city.

Earl says that during the summer of 1973, while they were living in Dallas, he had a dramatic UFO sighting. As with many of Earl's strange stories, there are two versions of the tale: his current memory of the event, and a contemporary account of it he had written in 1973. In this case, the contemporary account was completely forgotten until recently when Earl was searching through old papers for the poem about the Pillow Bandit and came across another poem of his describing the Dallas experience. Earl says he has no memory of having written about the Dallas sighting and the poem was a complete surprise to him when he happened across it in a file of other poems from that era. Fortunately, he told me about the sighting well before finding the forgotten manuscript, and, therefore, we can say with certainty that his current memory of it has not been influenced in any way by the content of the 1973 poem.

As Earl recalled the incident over the years, he was outside one summer day, working alone in the front yard of the Dallas farm, when he spotted an unknown object passing overhead at a high altitude. The object moved quickly, crossing the sky from horizon to horizon in a southerly direction in about five minutes. He wanted to go inside and get his telescope, but felt there wasn't enough time and that the object would be gone before he could set it up. As it turned out, he didn't need the telescope as the object was clearly visible to the naked eye—and what Earl saw was remarkable. He described it as:

> a large, bullet-shaped thing that had a rounded point on the front end and a flat or squared-off back end. There was heavy black smoke pouring out of the back of it, leavin g a trail. I didn't hear any sound, although it may have been too far away for the noise to carry. I had the impression that it was large, say the length of a jet liner, and thick, around twenty feet across. It really looked like a big, fat bullet. There were no wings visible, and no markings on it that I could see. The object was a dull color, possibly gray. No windows or other structural details were visible. The thing it most resembled is the spaceship in the Georges Méliès 1902 silent film *A TRIP TO THE MOON*. My younger brother had shown me an 8mm version of that film when I was in college, and I was reminded of the film when I saw the object. I think Jane was inside the house during my sighting, and that I excitedly came in afterward and told her about it. It didn't look like any known human aircraft.

Summarizing some of the key elements from his memory of the incident, this was a solitary, daylight sighting and Earl did not use his telescope to view the object.

The rediscovered 1973 poem "Enormous Flaming Thing In The Sky" tells a similar story, but with some major differences. In the poem, the poet attempts to view the object through the telescope, but can't find it due to the spotter scope being "bent" out of alignment and "fogged." While the shape of the object is not mentioned, it is said to have flames, not just smoke, coming from the back, and the tail is "detached," which probably means that the visible portion of the flame was offset from the exhaust pipe. Notably, the sighting takes place at night, with the moon rising above the trees, and there are two seasonal hints that the event happened in the fall, not the summer. One is the line comparing the moon to "a Harvest tune from an old folk song" and the other is the description of the telescope's spotter scope as being "fogged," implying its lens had condensation on it from the cool, damp autumn air. Lastly, the narrator is not alone, writing that, "We were looking at the moon."

Despite these differences, there are similarities between the two versions of the sighting. Both tell of an object that is at high altitude. "We watched it pass at a high arc," reads the poem. In both accounts, the object is large, "enormous" according to the poem. Both sightings take place at the Dallas farm, given the poem's reference to "the rooster atop Jane's barn," Jane, in this case, being a neighboring farmer, and not Earl's wife. And, in both accounts, the object is moving quickly, "too fast" according to the poem, implying that the object is an extraterrestrial craft, calling it "maybe one of them / Celestial Cars" and giving its origin as the vague "from hither & thither & who can say / which of God's Green Mansions." Oddly, in the line "Like unto a sputtering cinematographic / comet" the poem echoes Earl's association of the mysterious object with the ship in the Méliès film.

How to reconcile the differences in these two accounts of an unidentified object allegedly seen over Dallas, Oregon, in 1973? The simplest answer is that in the poem Heriot was employing poetic license, that he changed the facts to suit his own literary purposes. After all, it was a poem, not a UFO report. However, the specificity of the poem in some of its details (the misaligned spotter scope, for example) and the absence of any obvious fantasy elements, argue against the differences being due solely to poetic license. Earl says his telescope did have a misaligned spotter scope, and that there was in fact an iron rooster weathervane on top of the neighbor's barn.

Another more speculative explanation is that there may have been two sightings, not one: the first taking place in the summer when Earl was the only witness, and the second one occurring later that autumn when Jane also was a witness. If that's the case, for some reason Earl only retained conscious memory of the first sighting, with the second one wiped from his mind until it came to light again when the long lost poem was rediscovered.

This 1973 sighting was the only UFO-related or paranormal incident that Earl recalls happening until a couple years after he and Jane moved back to Southern California in 1978. For the approximately seven years following the Dallas sighting, he had no bizarre memories, no weird mental images, no unexplained paranormal events.

> All during those early years in Oregon, I never felt like there was anything "alien" or creepy hanging around on the fringes of my life. It was a very peaceful period.

In 1978, missing the friends they had made in college and the cultural richness of Southern California, Earl, his wife Jane, and their two young daughters packed up and moved back to Southern California, first living for about six months in Orange County, then moving again to Long Beach to be closer to the people and places that had lured them back south in the first place.

They were in the Long Beach rental for only a few months, forced to move once again when the landlord unexpectedly sold the property and it was scheduled to be torn down to make way for a new apartment building. At this point, they found a nice house to rent in Lakewood, the city where Earl grew up. Lakewood is adjacent to Long Beach, and thus it was still convenient for him in terms of staying connected with his old circle of friends. What he didn't know was that bizarre and disturbing experiences involving alien forces would resume upon his return to Lakewood.

Earl describes these new UFO-related experiences as "a complex series of events taking place over a period of about a year," beginning in 1981 and extending into 1982. For simplicity of discussion, they can be grouped into two main "stories"—one that he calls "the three vibrating spheres" story (that follows), and another dubbed "the Long Beach Blimp UFO" story (in chapter 7). As with some of his other stories, there are two versions of these tales: what Earl now consciously recalls from memory, and the story as documented by Earl in writing at the time of the event. Concerning the first story, Earl has reread his written narrative about it only once since it was composed, and that was many years ago. As for the second story, he has never reread the original account, which is quite lengthy and detailed. By his not being overly familiar with the documented version of each story, I am confident we are getting his pure "uncontaminated" memory of the event as it has persisted in his conscious mind over the intervening years. I interviewed Earl about his memories before he found these old writings and loaned them to me for examination.

THREE VIBRATING SPHERES

At the Lakewood rental, their two little girls slept in a small bedroom at the front of the house while Earl and Jane shared a den-type family room at the back of the house. This makeshift bedroom had sliding glass doors that opened onto a patio. The bed faced the glass doors, which Earl found "unnerving." Earl says that over a period that he guesses lasted a month or so, he had several bizarre "dreams" that consisted of seeing above him, high over the bed, a group of three metallic spheres that were suspended together in midair, in a tight triangular formation.

> They would vibrate and hum for a long time, and I had the impression they were transferring some sort of information to my brain. I never knew what it was they were "telling" me, so to speak.
>
> Around the same period, I started having what I can only describe as "electromagnetic bodily phenomena," as well as psychic powers. I discovered that I could be sitting across the room from the TV and just by raising my hand and pointing a finger at the set, I could make it have static interference, with "snow" or wavy lines filling the screen and the audio buzzing with random noise. It worked with all sorts of radios and televisions, and not just the ones in our house. I almost got myself into trouble at work one day when I demonstrated this unusual power for my boss. We were in his office, going over a report I'd drafted, and his radio was on his desk, playing softly. "Watch this!" I said. I pointed at the radio and it buzzed loudly, blocking out the music. When I lowered my finger, the music came back on and the buzzing stopped. He looked completely astounded. "How in the hell did you do that?" he

demanded. I quickly realized I'd made a mistake showing him this talent and decided to pass it off as a harmless parlor stunt. "It's a magic trick," I claimed. "Once you know the secret, it's easy. I'm not giving it away, though. You gotta figure it out for yourself." He let it go, but I could tell he was suspicious, and wasn't quite buying my story.

One evening I was out with a group of friends and suddenly discovered I had the ability to read the mind of someone at our table. I was sitting next to a woman who was a friend of a friend of mine. I happened to also know her because she often babysat for my wife while she was out running errands and I was at work. I knew hardly anything about this woman and nothing about her personal life other than the fact that she was married and had kids of her own. She lived down the street from us and I would chat with her briefly when I picked up the kids, but I never met her husband or heard her discussing their relationship. As far as I knew, she was happily married. But that evening, sitting there at the table with my friends, I could suddenly see into this woman's mind, her inner thoughts, her very being. It was all laid out for me to view. It's not like I wanted to read her mind—it was there, right in front of me, unavoidable. I should have just kept my mouth shut but instead I told her everything I perceived: the troubles she'd been having with her husband, various difficulties in her life, things that were making her sad, and she confirmed that it was all unfortunately true. She wanted to know how I could know all this private stuff about her, and all I could say was that, "I'm psychic sometimes and I just sense it, although I'm not trying to." She was totally blown away by the details I was able to tell her about herself and her life. This psychic "reading" of her thoughts and emotions went on for about a half-hour and then I left the bar we were at and headed for home. I told Jane about it and she thought it was very odd, but we soon forgot about it. I never again talked with the woman other than inconsequential small talk when I picked up the kids. It was only later that I came to suspect the electromagnetic effects I'd been experiencing and this single psychic episode might be related to those freaky dreams about the three vibrating metallic spheres.

That's how Earl remembers this particular series of events. Now let's look at what he wrote about it at the time.

The document in question is a five-page prose narrative that Earl self-published as a chapbook in 1985. Because it's a published work, to protect his privacy I'm not going to reveal its title. The narrative is in the form of a somewhat humorous meditative essay composed on Christmas Eve 1981. Earl writes about philosophical matters related to the meaning of life, the nature of reality, etc., and mentions—interestingly—experiments rumored to have been conducted by the Russians using electromagnetic force fields for the purpose of remote, long distance mind control over humans. However, Earl does not write about his own personal experiences wherein he physically affected the functioning of TV and radio devices without touching them. He also makes no mention of the mind-reading incident with the neighbor lady.

So far, this document is only indirectly related to the story of the three spheres. But then, towards the end of the chapbook, he describes a series of dreams he's had recently that are clearly the "dreams" he now remembers about the three spheres. He calls the dreams "very complex, difficult to describe." They feature three "focal points" that he speculates may represent electrical, magnetic, and gravitational forces. He goes on to say that the dreams usually transform into "lovely UFO images," one of which was a brilliant donut-shaped light positioned high in the sky that later burst into "numerous luminous disks" in a firework-like explosion. Most of the flaming embers from this explosion fell to the ground, but three of them formed into disc-shaped UFOs that spread out in the sky and flew off into the distance, disappearing over the Santa Monica Mountains.

Heriot then spends two paragraphs in his essay discussing different types of UFOs and aliens in general, but I have the impression that this is a rehash of material he's read in the ufology literature and not an account of any personal sightings or a revelation of any knowledge gained from firsthand experiences.

It's a curious little booklet, and you have to wonder what, other than compelling UFO dreams he actually did have, would have motivated him to write this piece? I believe it was his way of dealing with a set of disturbing experiences that he could barely understand, let alone fully describe. Its very existence argues for its likely authenticity as a document of paranormal or ufological phenomena. It should be noted that Heriot has no conscious memory of having seen any alien entities during this period—not even in dreams. Perhaps, if he did have such encounters, the memories are too deeply buried in his subconscious mind for him to recall without the aid of hypnotic regression, which he rejects.

CHAPTER SIX

GRAVE GRAYS

The two most common paranormal phenomena in the twenty-first century are the appearance of UFOs (and their occupants) and ghosts. Numerous television programs and books cover both subjects with entertainment and have captured viewers' and readers' attentions unlike any other scientifically unexplainable phenomenon. UFOs, aliens, and ghosts are difficult to document beyond eyewitness testimony. Videos and photos exist, but in the day of superb computer graphics, images of UFOs, aliens, and ghosts are becoming more difficult to discern fact from faked. I have never seen a photo or video of an alien that passed the "bullshit" test. Alien abductions provide researchers with more eyewitness testimony, usually under hypnotic regression. Alien implants discovered within abductees, scoop marks, punctures, and missing fetuses are testable, tangible evidence of abductions. UFO sightings are supported with radar data and, sometimes, trace evidence of a landing (including burn marks, higher than background radiation, electromagnetic anomalies, and

> "KIDS ALREADY HAVE MONSTERS UNDER THE BED, MONSTERS IN THE CLOSET—NOW THERE'S GRAYS BEHIND THE DRESSER?!"
>
> —UNDISCLOSED PARANORMAL RADIO SHOW HOST

changes to soil chemistry). Ghost hunters equip themselves with electromagnetic field (EMF) detection devices and electronic voice phenomena (EVP) recorders, sometimes catching what sound like messages from beyond. Rapid decreases in temperature are also noted as evidence of the presence of ghosts. Poltergeists disrupt a household with loud noises and objects thrown around or stacked as if by a haunt with obsessive compulsive disorder. Ectoplasm is defined as the thick mist that accompanies the appearance of a ghost, a substance that can be captured only photographically.

In many ways, ufology and the study of ghosts are very similar. Both phenomena challenge researchers with confounding paranormal high strangeness just on the fringes of science, glimpses of the unbelievable with few tools to confirm or deny their existence in our universe. Scientists are loathe to consider the paranormal as an actual manifestation in the natural universe. Many ufologists and ghost hunters are hesitant to recognize a commonality between aliens and ghosts, but the two phenomena share many features. Both quite often appear as orbs! Orbs have always been a very common form of UFO sighting and commonly appear prior to alien abduction. But how to know whether the orb is an alien or a ghost?

A comparison between Grays and ghosts follows, with similarities and differences noted between the two forms of entity:

SIMILARITY	GRAY	GHOST
1. EXHIBITS SHAPE OR FORM (ESPECIALLY "ORB")	X	X
2. CHANGES SHAPE OR FORM	X	X
3. LEVITATION	X	
4. TRANSPARENCY		X
5. MOVES THROUGH SOLID OBJECTS	X	X
6. APPEARS AND DISAPPEARS (VISUALLY)	X	X
7. TELEKINESIS (SPECIFICALLY, POLTERGEIST ACTIVITY)		X
8. APPEARS PRIMARILY AT NIGHT (WAKING AND DREAMING)	X	X
9. COMMUNICATES WITH PERSON (GRAY TELEPATHICALLY, GHOST TELEPATHICALLY OR AUDIBLE VOICE)	X	X
10. PHYSICALLY CONTROLS PERSON (GRAY FULL BODY PARALYSIS AND GHOST "POSSESSION")	X	X
11. PARANORMAL ACTIVITY ASSOCIATED WITH SPECIFIC PLACE (GRAY SERIAL ABDUCTIONS AND GHOST HAUNTING)	X	X

Certainly, this is not an exhaustive list, but it does begin a discussion of the "paraphysical" (as defined by Raymond Fowler) qualities associated with Grays and ghosts.

The Gray is instantly recognizable with its large teardrop-shaped head, huge black lens-shaped eyes, gangly body, and gray skin color; vertical in its physical orientation, and appearing to be a neonate humanoid. A ghost can take the form of a person. Both Grays and ghosts are capable of changing form, specifically into glowing orbs. Grays can levitate. Ghosts, too, are capable of levitation, but this is stretching the definition of the word since ghosts are intangible. Ghosts are often transparent, while Grays appear most often in a solid, biological state of being. Both Grays and ghosts are capable of moving through solid objects. The Gray "phases" its material body through doors, windows, etc. Ghosts are already intangible and pass through matter as continuously "phased" entities. Grays and ghosts can appear and disappear (visually) at will. Poltergeists are able to move solid objects with some form of telekinesis. Grays move objects with their bifurcated tentacles. Ghosts can be detected using EMF detectors. Grays do not exhibit EMF, but contact with UFOs often results in EMF disruption. Grays and ghosts are active primarily at night when people are sleeping, and often appear in dreams and the intermediate state between dream and consciousness. Grays communicate with people via telepathy. Ghosts can be heard telepathically or audibly (especially with the use of EVP recorders). Grays physically control people with some form of paralysis field. Ghosts can enter a person and "possess" the body, allowing the ghost to speak through a person and control mobility. Grays are often associated with a specific place, usually wherever the abductee happens to reside. Ghosts haunt specific places, somehow trapped in the physical realm where their body died or was tormented.

Are these paraphysical qualities an indication of a true relation between Grays and ghosts, or do both entities simply share these characteristics as separate phenomena? My guess is that a true relation exists between Grays and ghosts, that both have a common origin in the same paranormal source. Human beings have been aware of "the other side" for at least 40,000 years, as evidenced by shamanic Paleolithic cave art. To the shaman, the cave wall is a membrane between this world and the world of the unseen. Power from the other side is transferred to the shaman while in an altered state of consciousness deep in the cave, and then shared with the people outside the cave in the light of day. This power increases the probability of a successful hunt, and gives ecto-political power to the shaman. You could reasonably assert, archaeologically, that this ritualistic behavior was the invention of religion. You might also conclude that this was the human discovery of "the other side." Both interpretations are valid. The origin of aliens and ghosts, then, can be said to come from "the other side." But what does this mean?

"The other side" is another reality beyond our conscious waking experience of existence. It is the origin of all that is paranormal and almost entirely beyond the scope of modern science. I say "almost" because quantum physics can predict other realities, a multiverse. Manifestations of the paranormal slide from one reality to another, probably inhabiting an infinity of alternate realities, including our waking state reality, yet stubbornly confounding the scientific method. I am not even sure that the scientific method should always be attempted in the study of the paranormal. The scientific method is a strict tool of inquiry into the natural universe. Its limits are rigidly defined, and any phenomenon that cannot be tested for confirmation or denial is automatically excluded from the realm of scientific investigation. The scientific method is quite often the wrong tool for the job of understanding and testing the paranormal. Paranormal investigators invent or adapt their own investigative tools. But what are the rules? Science is dominated by rational rules. How can the paranormal be investigated, systematically and reliably, if not by immutable laws? Perhaps the laws are not broken by the paranormal—maybe the paranormal brings to light new laws.

What if, hypothetically, the paranormal cannot be tested in any way scientifically? Maybe the scientific tools for poking in the darkness have proven inadequate to the job. I have argued elsewhere that ufology can be tested scientifically, and MUFON's Mission Statement explicitly calls for scientific inquiry. This is good, but insufficient by itself to understand the greater high strangeness. The same applies to ghosts—study of the paranormal most often cannot be tested with repeatability. Hypotheses of the paranormal will never lead to scientifically supported theories because a scientific theory requires many fruitful hypotheses that have been tested again and again and never been refuted. UFOs, aliens, and ghosts very rarely, if at all, reappear in a controlled setting. They do not allow for the scientific method to produce anything more than correlations. We have no causation because we do not really understand, at all, what is causing the phenomena. But just because something cannot be tested scientifically does not make it any less real or significant than scientific knowledge. Poetry, for example, cannot be tested using the scientific method. Any results would be worthless and absurd. Literary analysis is the tool for understanding poetry.

Are investigations into UFOs, aliens, and ghosts primarily "paranormal analysis"? This sidestep away from science immediately releases ufology from its apologetic position to proactive paranormal study, and investigators already use tools for paranormal analysis within the context of each paranormal field. If UFO researchers perform paranormal analysis, then ufologists can ignore those who belittle them, like Bill Nye and Neil deGrasse Tyson. They will continue to demean UFO researchers with their pronouncements that ufology is not scientific, and ufologists can reply with full confidence, "Many phenomena in our universe are real yet unscientific. What's your point?" because if their point is that scientific knowledge is the best knowledge, we can expose their prejudice for what it is—a single-minded attack on the unscientific. Most people do not approach life according to strict scientific principles. Ufology uses scientific instruments and has at least produced interesting studies in the humanities. Furthermore, the goal of attempting scientifically to approach primarily the UFO question has actually led to some startling conclusions (especially noted in Paul Hill's *Unconventional Flying Objects*).

UFO craft and inhabitants often appear as if they are real and "unreal" simultaneously, more like projections than physical objects. Ghosts exhibit the same quality. The fact that both have been captured photographically in orb form suggests a similar mode of existence, perhaps precisely the same form, at least while the Gray or ghost is traveling. Again, how to know whether the orb is an alien or a ghost? I agree with Raymond Fowler (in his book *The Watchers II*) that "paraphysical" phenomena all share their origin in death. My conception of death is contradictory, however. What is death? My first response is that death is exactly the same as what you are experiencing right now, only you are not alive to experience it. Yet death is also "the other side," "the undiscovered country," the origin of everything "unreal." I can accept this contradiction in my worldview, in fact, actively encourage diverse, opposing opinions competing and co-developing in my mind, and ultimately resulting in a narrative to explain, or at least describe, the paranormal. Shared narratives of paranormal phenomena fill volumes, this book being but one example. High strangeness occurs, is recorded and shared with the greater community of paranormal investigators, and increases the knowledge base of correlations between phenomena, such as UFOs and ghosts. The shared narrative of the paranormal opens up further the unreal for paranormal analysis.

JUDY AND MAX MANCHESTER

Consider the following case of Judy Manchester's poltergeist activity in Madison, Wisconsin. Compared to other poltergeist activity, the following may seem tame, but it is still unexplainable and exhibits high strangeness.

JORDAN HOFER (JH): When did this strange activity begin?

JUDY MANCHESTER (JM): Probably sometime in 1974 when my husband and son and I lived in an old two-story house in Madison, Wisconsin.

JH: What was the first incident that struck you as odd?

JM: I believe that would have to be the phantom footsteps we heard at the front door: a loud clomping like someone beating dirt off his boots. When we opened the door, no one was there and there was no evidence of anyone or anything having been there.

JH: How long did this continue?

JM: Oh, probably for about two years.

JH: And you never found an explanation?

JM: No. There was never anyone at the door, even when we opened it quickly after the loud noise, and it was loud!

JH: What other strange occurrences do you remember?

JM: I remember one night, I had just put my son to sleep, and my husband and I were up late watching television. Suddenly, there was a loud crashing, like glass shattering, from the basement. My husband grabbed a butcher knife and I got a flashlight and a frying pan. We looked in every corner and cranny of that basement and nothing, absolutely nothing, had fallen or crashed, and there was no one down there. In fact, there was nothing in that basement but a washer and drier.

JH: Is it possible you only thought the sound came from the basement? Might it have originated from someplace else?

JM: No. The loud crashing sound came from the basement, nowhere else.

JH: Do you have any idea what caused the noise?

JM: No. But I never felt comfortable in the basement. I always had a strange feeling about it.

JH: What else happened?

JM: The only other strange thing was the silverware and the dishes.

JH: Strange in what way?

JM: Only my husband and son and I lived in the house. We rarely had friends over. Usually we were invited to a friend's place. My son was just a toddler and could not have reached either the silverware drawer or the dishes. Also, my husband and I were very honest with each other. We would tease each other, but we never played tricks on each other or pulled hoaxes.

JH: So what happened with the silverware and dishes?

JM: It was the damnedest, strangest thing! I had washed and dried the silverware and put it away very neatly in a drawer. I am very tidy in the kitchen. About an hour after I had put away the silverware, I went to get a spoon, and the drawer was a mess! Spoons, forks, knives, all mixed up, like someone had just taken an armload of them and dumped them into the drawer! This made me really mad because, as I said, I like a very neat kitchen. I knew my son hadn't done it because he was too young and couldn't reach the drawer, so I asked my husband if he was playing a trick on me. He was just as perplexed as I was, and even thought that I was playing a joke on him! I have no idea how the silverware got messed up. Then, just the next day, the plates were rattling loudly in the cabinet. Only the plates. When I heard them, I thought perhaps we were having a small earthquake or something, but nothing else was shaken and I felt no vibrations.

JH: When you consider all of these strange things that happened, what do you think caused it?

JM: (Laughs) Oh, for silly! I'm an atheist and I don't believe in ghosts. But I guess you want me to say it was a poltergeist, don't you, Jordy?

Judy Manchester's poltergeist activity included the production of loud noises without a causative source, similar to EVP. The rattling of her dishes and the mess of silverware can be attributed to telekinesis, which is often associated with poltergeists. Try to consider this true story from a scientific perspective. Can it be repeated? No. Can it be confirmed or denied? No. It is impossible to use the scientific method to understand this anecdote, primarily because it is an anecdote, an occurrence that is not repeatable or testable scientifically. This does not negate the truth of the story, however. Judy was able, automatically, to apply "paranormal analysis" from a greater knowledge base of just such occurrences, and identify the possible source as a poltergeist. Culturally, as if by oral tradition from our pre-recorded history, people generally know what a poltergeist is and what activity to expect from one.

According to Reverend John H. Hampsch (in his booklets *Devils and Demons: Fact or Fiction?* and his much expanded *Poltergeists and Seven Types of Ghosts*):

> Poltergeists are not humans but devilishly mischievous evil spirits; they're mostly rather stupid, and in the hierarchy of the nefarious, they're the underlings of the underworld.

Judy's son, Max Manchester, recalls strange memories from the poltergeist haunted house:

JORDAN HOFER (JH): Do you remember the poltergeist?

MAX MANCHESTER (MM): No, not the poltergeist. But I remember, nightly, when the closet door opened and Greco-Roman statues filed out and into my room. Marble, some missing limbs. How could a two-year-old know enough about Greco-Roman sculptures to imagine a nightly procession from his closet?

JH: Do you think the statues were ghosts?

MM: No. I think they were alien screen memories. Grays.

JH: Why would they disguise themselves as Greco-Roman statues?

MM: Maybe because they're creepy.

JH: You lived in a house with both poltergeist and alien activity?

MM: I don't believe there was any poltergeist.

JH: What do you believe?

MM: I know all of it was the Grays.

Max Manchester also revealed to me another "haunting" he experienced at the age of twelve.

MM: I used to sleep-over at my friend Jake's house. He had this big bunk bed even though he was an only child. I always slept on the bottom bunk. The weird thing is that every time I slept over, the bed would rock at precisely 11:23 p.m.
JH: What do you mean by "the bed would rock"?

MM: It shook. The whole heavy frame of the bunk bed was shaking.
JH: How many times did you witness this?

MM: I don't know. Several, I guess. But Jake said it was a regular nightly occurrence—at precisely 11:23 p.m.
JH: Do you have any idea what made the bed rock or shake?

MM: Not unless Jake was shaking it, but I don't see how he could. He denied it. I believe him. He told me that the previous family who lived in his house had a baby that died, and that Jake's bedroom had been the baby's bedroom.
JH: So, Jake thought he was being haunted by a dead baby?

MM: He was convinced the baby had died at 11:23 p.m. and that the shaking of the bed was the baby rocking in its crib.
JH: What do you think it was?

MM: The Grays, obviously.

JUDD FARMER

The next case is very strange and includes four witnesses on four separate occasions in an old Victorian home in Portland, Oregon in 1997. Judd Farmer was the first to encounter the ghost.

JORDAN HOFER (JH): You said you actually heard the ghost?
JUDD FARMER (JF): Yes. I was sleeping upstairs in the study when I heard a loud, agonized moaning. It woke me up immediately and I was terrified.

JH: You said you were sleeping. How do you know this was not just a dream?
JF: Well, I guess I can't be a hundred percent sure of that. But I wasn't the only one to hear it. One of my roommates heard it, too.

JH: The same night?
JF: No, not the same night. Sometime later. It woke him up, too.

JH: So, you both could have dreamed it?
JF: Maybe. But my other roommate heard it a month later, and he wasn't sleeping.

JH: What did he hear, precisely?
JF: A loud moaning, like a man in pain.

JH: From where in the house did the moaning originate?
JF: On the first floor, in the front room.

JH: And all three of you were upstairs when you heard it?
JF: Yeah.

JH: What else happened? You told me four people witnessed the ghost.
JF: The last person to "witness" it was a friend of ours who didn't live with us. One night he came over and, as he walked up the front steps, he saw through the window an old man sitting in one of the recliners. He thought my roommate's dad had come to visit. When he came inside, the old man was gone.

JH: So, it wasn't your roommate's father?
JF: No, he wasn't there that night. And like I said, the old man was gone when our friend came inside.

JH: Did anyone else see the old man?
JF: No. Just our friend.

JH: Were there any other "encounters" with the old man?
JF: No, that was the last one. But we did find out who he was.

JH: Really?
JF: Yeah. There was a really nice old lady who lived to the right of us. We would talk occasionally over the fence. One day I told her about everything that we had heard and seen of the ghost. She told me that, before we had moved in, the Victorian house had belonged to an old man who was very sick and in chronic pain. He killed himself in the front room with a plastic bag over his head.

JH: So your neighbor believed you?
JF: Oh, yeah. She was convinced the house was haunted.

JH: What do you think?
JF: That it was haunted. Definitely.

The first two encounters with the old man's ghost may only have been nightmares, but two were experienced in a conscious state. If they were hallucinations, auditory and visual, then they were very "lifelike" and convincing. The power of place in this case is very strong, especially located in the front room where the old man committed suicide with a plastic bag. The old man's agony was paraphysically entwined with the house. Death by carbon dioxide poisoning is not painless.

JACK PAULSON

Jack Paulson understands the power of place in paranormal activity after having lived on the unofficial reservation of the Klamath Tribe in Chiloquin, Oregon, for two years. He believes the entire town and area are haunted.

JORDAN HOFER (JH): The whole town is haunted?
JACK PAULSON (JP): Actively, yes. The entire area: the houses, the river and its bank, the dusty streets, the train tracks. And the pentacles. That's what Mike called them. Mike was a Klamath Indian I used to drink and smoke with. He said there were pentacles all over Chiloquin. As far as I could understand, a "pentacle" was the spirit of someone who was attracted to a specific place.

JH: Did you ever encounter one of these "pentacles"?
JP: One night, yes, without doubt. I was sleeping in the front den when I heard the voice of a kindly old lady say, "Hello." Somehow I could see her outside, beyond the front window. She was tiny, bent over, and looked Native American. I got up and went to where my wife was sleeping in the next room, only she wasn't in bed. She was standing up and bent over. I asked her what she was doing. She said that she was helping the old woman to stand and walk. When we woke up the next morning we compared notes. Both of us had seen and heard an old Indian woman—we had shared a dream of her at the same time! So I asked our landlord if an old Indian woman had ever lived in the house. He was surprised as he answered yes. I told him about the simultaneous dreams. "She was a sweet old Indian lady," said the landlord. "She was in the hospital but came home here to die. She loved this house. Next time you see her, say hello for me." I had Mike over for some wine. He chanted some songs in Klamath. I asked him about the old woman who died in the house and he spoke of her reverentially, and told me that her pentacle was very strong in the house.

JH: Did you ever see or hear her ghost again?
JP: No. But she was there. We shared the house with her. I always felt safe there. But Mike was more dangerous than I thought. While I was on vacation out of town, Mike got really drunk one night and killed his friend John over a bottle of booze. John's pentacle is in a bushy area on the river bank. Never did see or hear him, but I knew he was there where Mike killed him.

JH: You said the whole area was haunted?
JP: Yeah, there were pentacles everywhere in Chiloquin. When I heard and saw the old woman that night, I realized that "white man's rules" didn't apply in Chiloquin. How many thousands of years was that area settled by the First Americans? I was taken by members of the tribe to a secret location along the river to see ancient rock art. The medicine man gave me tobacco to offer the holy places. Some of the rock art had been "strengthened" recently with orange spray paint. The medicine man was also a cultural anthropologist. He explained to me that the spray paint was not graffiti, but that another medicine man was maintaining the vitality of the ancient symbols. I definitely felt the strength

of that place, powerful with not just culture, but spirit.

JH: Did you ever feel out of place in the face of such strong cultural resonance?

JP: The Klamath spirit blanketed Chiloquin in years of deeply cherished tradition. The pentacles kept watch over the town. I was an interloper, a mild intruder.

Place can be potent with power, whether on Native American soil, in a haunted house, or the cold white surfaces of an alien operating theater.

BENJAMIN JEFFRIES

I asked Benjamin Jeffries, paranormal investigator and author of *Lost in the Darkness*, what he thought about the zone of convergence between aliens and ghosts:

Some see no correlation between the two. The world of spirits is a human belief, and the alien presence is more of an interplanetary belief. That line which connects Alien Contact with Ghostly Contact is very thin and narrow, replete with too many complex answers to fairly simple questions. Alien beings and human beings are, with the exception of a few oddly placed chromosomes and molecules, living beings that live on energy, thrive on it, and expel it when death occurs. If a living human can become a ghost or energy-driven spirit, what is to stop an alien being from doing the same once it expires? Numerous psychic mediums, from Edgar Cayce to Amy Allan, have recorded encounters with the spirits of alien beings during states of meditation or communication with the dead. If it lives, it breathes. If it breathes, it creates, uses, and stores energy. If it dies, that energy is expelled as the person or being's essence or spirit. Take the phenomenon of alien abduction. Victim is awake, paralyzed in their bed, with several creatures surrounding them. Then, in the next moment, they are in a ship with bright lights, usually lying on a table, still paralyzed. This same scenario has been described by victims of ghostly visitations, only instead of being surrounded by aliens, the victim is surrounded by a black mass or a fearsome, demonic-looking entity. Paralysis almost always accompanies both of these scenarios and plays a fairly major role in the victim's forced subservience.

Is it coincidence that the two scenarios seem similar? Is it possible that, while the human entities can only visit the living, the alien entities have mastered the theoretical art of projecting their spirits to make infiltration into the locked home easier? And with the mastery of this projection, isn't it possible that they can essentially take the victim with them and return him or her just as easily? The skeptic would even point to the idea of Night Terrors being the true culprit for BOTH scenarios, with the very real Sleep Paralysis Disorder at its main core. But one thing a skeptic can't do is empathize with those that have experienced these visitations. To empathize would lend credence to such an idea, so a skeptic's mind must remain closed in order to maintain its stance in the face of opposition. This restrains the skeptic from exploring a world of incredible possibilities and he remains locked in a windowless room.

I agree that ghosts and Grays are very similar in their appearance (as orbs) and behaviors (hauntings and abductions); also, some orbs may very well be Grays and, as Benjamin Jeffries astutely points out in his statement, ghosts. I do not believe I have ever heard this idea posited. As if Grays and ghosts weren't creepy enough, now we may very well be haunted by Gray ghosts! Leave it to Benjamin Jeffries to turn creepy up to eleven! Alien visitation is haunting on a planetary scale!

CHAPTER SEVEN

THE LONG BEACH BLIMP UFO

O ver three decades later, Earl Heriot consciously recalls a second UFO-related experience during the period when he and his family were living in Lakewood. While he doesn't remember the exact date, he says it happened a few months after the "three vibrating spheres" dreams.

I was working at a research firm in Santa Monica and commuting several hours a day on the 405 Freeway. My route went right by the Goodyear Blimp Base Airport in Carson, California, and I would often spot the blimp either moored on the field or up in the air, coming and going. There was nothing unusual about seeing the blimp, and I was very accustomed to it. However, one afternoon as I was driving south on my way home from work, I spotted the blimp low in the air, not far away, over on the left side of the freeway. It was right there as I was just about to pass it, and then suddenly—BAM!—in the blink of an eye, it was far away, a mile or so down the freeway, still on the left side. It was as if the blimp had instantaneously "leaped ahead" from one position to another. *THAT'S REALLY WEIRD!* I thought. I may have even said it out loud, although I was alone in the car. A minute or two later, I again approached the blimp—which all along had been cruising at a modest speed of about thirty miles per hour except during its "leap ahead" move—and was about to pull up level with it and pass it, when the blimp again jumped ahead of me, and was suddenly another mile or two down the road. It was freaky, like the thing was intentionally playing cat and mouse with me. I wondered if other drivers noticed this weird behavior or if I was the only one. At some point, I became aware that the electronic reader board sign on the side of the blimp was displaying a strange set of symbols or hieroglyphics instead of its usual mundane messages in English. "What the hell?" I muttered.

At this point, I began to suspect that I was watching a UFO and not a conventional aircraft. While I had assumed it was the familiar Goodyear Blimp, I don't think I had actually seen the word "Goodyear" on it. Its color was dark, almost solid black, and not the blue, silver, and yellow theme for which the blimp was famous. The object had the profile of a blimp, with a large oval body and a gondola cabin on the underside.

Earl found the manuscript that he wrote in 1983 describing his experiences with the blimp-like UFO. Given the bizarre nature of those experiences, which Earl describes in great detail, the entire document is presented below. Shortly after he completed the first draft of this narrative, Earl went through it "marking out passages that seemed too weird to be true." While he insists that he sought to be completely honest in telling this story, after the fact, his "logical," conscious mind found some of it too incredible to accept as reality. He decided to delete the more fantastic parts and publish only whatever matter-of-fact information remained after this act of self-censorship. Nonetheless, ultimately, he feared that even a sanitized version of the story would jeopardize his reputation as a credible person, and thus he decided not to publish any of it. Thankfully, Earl did not destroy the document, and it has survived for our consideration and analysis.

In the following transcription of the manuscript, passages that Earl had marked for deletion because he felt they "went too far" or were "too revealing" are kept intact. I preserve a few of his minor deletions that seem more a matter of writing style than self-censorship, and in other cases I ignore his minor changes when the original text seems stylistically better. I've also corrected errors in spelling and grammar.

THE LONG BEACH AIRPORT FLYING SAUCER SIGHTINGS OF 1982

One evening, two years ago, while driving home from work along the busy San Diego Freeway in Southern California, I saw an "Unidentified Flying Object," a UFO, at close range.

This was in mid-February 1982, and although I didn't realize it at the time, Long Beach was in the middle of a small UFO flap. The saucers were being sighted by multiple, apparently independent, witnesses in the vicinity of the Long Beach Airport. I was living in the area at the time and happened to witness the phenomenon on several occasions.

I was then employed as an economic research analyst for a private consulting firm located in Santa Monica, about thirty miles northwest of Long Beach. I was living in Lakewood, a small suburban city bordering Long Beach. My daily sixty-mile round-trip commute to and from work via the San Diego Freeway brought me past the Long Beach Airport twice a day.

It was during the drive home one evening about 6:30 p.m., shortly after sunset, that I first saw the UFO. I'm uncertain of the exact date or the day of the week of this first sighting, as the event did not fully register in my conscious mind (as I will soon explain) but I think it was probably Wednesday, February 17, 1982. I am sure that it was during the week of February 15th to February 22nd. The sky was a deep shade of purple and I seem to recall the weather was clear, without rain, fog or overcast. [Editor: Historical weather records confirm there was no precipitation in Long Beach during that period.]

I was just entering Long Beach, headed east, with the Long Beach Municipal Airport up ahead on my left, and the setting sun behind me, over my right shoulder. As I came to within a mile or so of the airport, I noticed a large aerial object to my left, north of the freeway and quite a distance ahead of me.

The object itself was dark, but discernible against the night sky. It was clearly some type of artificial, constructed craft, as opposed to a natural object or an optical illusion. Its "running lights" were unusually dim.

I assumed it was the famous Goodyear Blimp, which operates out of an airfield located about seven miles to the northwest, in the City of Carson. It didn't seem extraordinary to see the blimp over Long Beach, as I was accustomed to spotting it all up and down the freeway from Long Beach to the South Bay area. Thus, at first, I paid only casual attention to the object.

When I came to within a half-mile west of the airport, I saw the object had crossed over to the south side of the freeway, still quite some distance ahead of my car. I was traveling about sixty mph, and for safety's sake only took my eyes off the road for a moment at a time to glance up at the peculiar looking "blimp."

By the time I reached the airport, the object was on my right side, about a fourth of a mile away, hovering above Long Beach General Hospital at a low altitude of 500 feet or so. As usual, I had the radio on and the car windows rolled up, so I can't say if it made any noise at all.

At some point between its passing over the freeway and its subsequent coming to rest in the airspace above the hospital, I came to the realization that there was something highly peculiar about the object. It had a look to it that I can only describe as "eerie." I distinctly remember thinking: *THE GOODYEAR BLIMP SURE LOOKS WEIRD TONIGHT.*

Although I was driving at high speed along a busy freeway, I was able to take several quick glimpses at the UFO. To the best of my judgment, it had become fixed in a stationary position directly above the hospital, which was approximately a fourth of a mile from my car. The object was about 150 feet long and about fifty feet high. The main body of the craft was shaped much like a football: a huge elongated oval with bluntly pointed ends. The surface of the object was a flat, non-reflective black, and the object was discernible only as a silhouette against the lighter evening sky. One or two rows of evenly spaced circular red lights ran horizontally along the length of the object. These red lights were very dim, considering the size of the object, and were not nearly as bright as normal aircraft running lights. With such poor visibility, it seemed to me, the craft presented a serious hazard to the many small private planes that were constantly taking off and landing at the airport.

Other than the row of red lights and the general outline of its shape, no other features were distinguishable on the main body of the object. However, a large gondola-like cabin hung from beneath the object. About fifty feet long and ten feet tall, this cabin area was more brightly lit than the rest of the object, and its features were more distinct.

A soft, yellow glow came from inside the cabin. The structure was polygonal in shape, consisting of several equal-sized trapezoidal windows which formed its walls. These large windows were separated by some kind of thin framework. The cabin was sufficiently illuminated, the windows transparent, and I recall electronic lights and equipment on a panel and some occupants in the cabin. I soon passed the hospital and the object was no longer in my sight.

This entire first sighting did not last more than a minute or two. The shape, features, and lighting of the object remained constant throughout the episode. The lights neither flashed, nor did they change in color or intensity.

I should also mention that there were no vehicle interference effects: the radio didn't show any signs of interference or static, and the car engine wasn't affected by the proximity of the UFO. I mention these aspects of the encounter as an afterthought, for I didn't think of the object as a UFO during the first sighting. It seems odd to me that I didn't realize I was seeing a UFO, as I was already familiar with the subject at the time, having had a long-term interest in the "flying saucer" mystery. I've occasionally read books on UFOs since childhood, and had given much thought to the question of their reality, origins, and purposes over the years. Furthermore, I had experienced, for no apparent reason, a sudden heightening of interest, a burst of enthusiasm for the topic during the preceding summer, and had been reading every UFO-related book I could get my hands on.

My new enthusiasm for the UFO phenomenon peaked in November and December of 1982 [Editor: This appears to be an error by Earl. He probably meant December 1981], two months before this initial sighting, during which time I experienced a series of vivid, visionary dreams concerning UFOs, alien entities, and, for some reason, the interrelationships between electromagnetic force fields, gravity, and the time-space continuum. This later aspect of my UFO dreams was inexplicable to me, as I have only an average knowledge and awareness of physics. The intensity of these dreams, and their sometimes frightening nature, soon began to act as a drain on my nerves, and I had rapidly come to feel burned-out on the whole subject, experiencing a strong aversion to the UFO topic during January of 1982.

However, at the time I first saw the object in mid-February, I was not looking for or thinking about UFOs, but I thought I was well prepared to recognize a UFO if I saw one.

Nonetheless, I did not recognize what I saw that evening as a UFO. Furthermore, the sighting seemed to have almost no impact on my consciousness; as I said earlier, for some reason it just did not "register" with me. Not only did I ignore what I saw, I instantly forgot that I had even seen it.

Later, after I finally consciously remembered the event, I began to wonder why I didn't pull off the freeway at the nearest off-ramp and stop my car so that I could get a better look at the thing. That would have been the obvious thing for a "UFO buff" to do. Yet, it never occurred to me. I also wondered how many other drivers on the San Diego Freeway that night ignored or failed to recognize the UFO, or if they even saw it at all.

Much after the fact, I've theorized that perhaps the controlling agency of the UFO had affected a form of mind control over whatever witnesses were in the area, so as to pass more or less unnoticed among us.

Some form of mind control exerted over all humans in the area while the UFO was present might possibly explain my utter lack of response to what I saw. The only other logical reason I can think of to explain my lack of cognition of the UFO is a psychological one: perhaps, despite my long-term interest in the phenomenon, I wasn't yet mentally able to fully accept the idea of a UFO displaying itself and therefore I was blocking the shocking reality from full consciousness. My misidentification of the object as the Goodyear Blimp was a feeble attempt to normalize what I was seeing. Or, maybe the mind control I suspect may have been in effect included, as part of its mechanism, a tendency of witnesses to identify the object as some common aircraft, such as the Goodyear Blimp.

Whether self-inflicted or externally induced, my amnesia concerning the event was instant and complete. I arrived home, on time, without any thought that something out of the ordinary had happened on the freeway that night.

Later in the same week, I had one or more similar sightings. The subliminal nature of these sightings was such that, to this day, I can't remember exactly how many times I saw the object that week, but I do know that it was at least twice, and possibly three times more, after the initial sighting. The additional sightings occurred on a Wednesday, Thursday, and/or Friday night. My recollection of them is still cloudy, but I do remember that I saw the same object (or another identical one) hovering motionlessly over the hospital, in the same position that I had seen it before. It was approximately the same time of day, after sunset between 6:30 and 6:45 p.m. All factors including distance, shape, size and lighting were identical to the first sighting. The weather was clear and visibility was good in all instances.

The object remained in a fixed position throughout these secondary sightings, whereas it moved from one side of the freeway to the other during the first sighting. Incidentally, I don't believe I ever actually saw it in motion, even during the first sighting. It had merely changed position between glimpses.

The secondary sightings were also from my moving car, again, at about sixty mph. As usual, I was alone, and I didn't seem to register the UFO. I do recall saying to myself: *THERE IT IS AGAIN.*

For some reason, my amnesia is stronger with these secondary sightings and I can only summon up a vague mental image of the UFO.

Perhaps at this point I ought to discuss my emotional perceptions of the UFO, after the fact. These are feelings I have had about the UFO in recollection, and are not a part of my original conscious impression of what I saw. I have a strong feeling that what I saw may have been some sort of projection, either a physical projection of an image into the sky, such as a three-dimensional hologram, which would have been visible to one and all who happened to be looking up at that time, or perhaps a mental image, projected directly into the minds of whatever witnesses were on hand. Furthermore, if the UFO image was a mental event and not a physical one, it may have been selectively projected to target witnesses, including myself, for reasons known only to the UFO intelligences.

There was a most unusual quality to the image of the UFO that makes me wonder about its material reality. There were several out-of-the-ordinary visual aspects to the sightings. Although I was close to the UFO and perceived it stereoscopically (in 3-D), there was a certain flatness or insubstantiality to the image, as if the object were not a real part of its surrounding scene. It seemed a bit more chimerical than it should have if it were an ordinary aircraft. And the light emitted by the object is best described by terms such as "unearthly," "unnatural," "eerie" and "otherworldly."

On a deeper and less rational level, I have an impression of the object as somehow "sinister," as if it did not belong there in the sky above the hospital, and perhaps as if it were up to no good. This is somehow countered in my mind by the reassurance (from what source?) that it's okay. I have two impressions in this regard: one is that "they" (the occupants or guiding intelligences) are "scientists," or at least technicians, and that they're there to do a job. According to this impression, the UFO's presence was a matter-of-fact, everyday event, although of course, in truth, it was a most bizarre circumstance. The second impression stems from the first, and it is an admonishment for me to ignore the UFO, to dismiss it from my mind and let it go about its business.

My memory of what the occupants looked like is that they were taller than humans, about seven feet, male, humanoid in form, with large, bald heads and widely spaced oval or elliptical-shaped eyes. They had light gray, ash-like skin, and were dressed in a silvery gray uniform, much like a pilot's jumpsuit. I can picture some form of pleating or soft tubing across the chest of the suit, horizontally. The occupants were staring out through the windows, with lighted computer-like devices or wall maps behind them, on a central hub-like portion of the gondola room.

These "impressions" came to mind at different lengths of time after that first week of multiple, repressed sightings. The first, the "projection" hypothesis, was the earliest one, forming itself in my mind within a week or two, while the second impression, which involves the sinister intent versus the innocuous intent, along with the admonishment to forget, came to mind later, about a month afterward. While the last impression, the occupant image, was much slower to emerge, taking about six months to surface. Possibly, this suggests a gradual recollection of deeply buried or suppressed perceptions, possibly of telepathically received information.

As I've already stated, I seem to have had complete amnesia regarding the UFO after each of the sightings during that week in mid-February 1982. As far as I was concerned, it had been a normal workweek, no different than any other. I probably never would have remembered the sightings if my memory hadn't been accidentally jogged by a chance hearing of related UFO reports on a popular local radio program that very weekend.

It was 10:00, on Saturday night, and I was listening to Bill Jenkins' radio talk show program, *OPEN MIND*. My wife and I had seen a demonstration of a Tesla Coil at the Griffith Park Planetarium in Los Angeles, and it had aroused our interest in its legendary inventor, electrical engineering genius Nikola Tesla, the prototypical "mad scientist." While a discussion of Tesla's work is outside the scope of this work, suffice to say that Tesla is noted for his eccentric, unconventional approaches to the physical sciences and for his brilliance as a mechanical inventor. Tesla's concepts concerning matter and energy are still considered crackpot notions by some scientists, although a growing number of them are beginning to take a serious second look at his ideas. Bill Jenkins, the talk show host, was an avid Tesla supporter and often brought up Tesla's concepts during discussions about UFOs. One night, shortly after our visit to the planetarium, my wife happened to tune into the *OPEN MIND* show on her radio while driving home from work and was surprised to hear Tesla being discussed. It was still on when she arrived home. "Turn on the radio," she said. "They're talking about Tesla." I tuned in the station on the FM radio and was fascinated. Soon I was a regular listener.

I had been tape-recording the *OPEN MIND* show for several weeks, as Bill Jenkins had promised to bring on a noted authority on UFOs for a discussion of the "crashed saucer syndrome." I was still on the fence about the reality or non-reality of UFOs at that time, and therefore I was very interested in any information pertaining to physical, objective evidence of the nuts and bolts reality of UFOs as machines. So, I happened to record the program on that Saturday night following the week of my "forgotten" sightings.

Bill Jenkins' guest that night was Dr. J. Allen Hynek, a leading authority on the UFO phenomenon. The two men were talking about UFOs in general when Jenkins mentioned that he had received seven or eight reports during the week of an unidentified flying object seen over the Long Beach Airport. The calls were coming from apparently independent witnesses, all of whom described the same general sort of object: a large, oval object with red and amber lights underneath. According to the witnesses, the object was soundless and motionless. Observers also reported that the low-altitude craft was seen at close range, and that the amber lights on the underside of the craft were periodically turned on and off. I hadn't noticed any such change in the illumination from the object, but that could have been due to the fact that my sightings were each very short in duration, a minute or two at the most. Other than the flashing on and off of the object's lights, the description was identical to what I had seen. [Editor: Earl does not currently remember the craft as having amber lights, only red ones. However, in a fragmentary portion of Earl's 1983 manuscript, he describes the gondola windows as giving off a pale amber light. Earl's description of the UFO he saw thus closely agrees with the public reports he heard about on the Bill Jenkins radio show.]

My interest was immediately piqued by Bill Jenkins' summary of the UFO reports he had received. It was thrilling to think that a minor flying saucer flap was occurring at that moment only a mile from my home. Maybe, I thought, I'd even get a chance to see a UFO myself.

An instant later, I realized that I had seen one. Suddenly, the suppressed image of the UFO I had witnessed earlier that week came sharply to mind. I had seen it and not even remembered, and I had seen it more than once. But why had I forgotten it? Why didn't I realize immediately that it was a true UFO?

When the program went off the air at midnight, I rewound the tape and listened to the part about the Long Beach sightings, comparing the description of the UFO as passed on by Bill Jenkins from his witnesses' reports with the object I had seen. It seemed as if there were no differences between the two, other than the fact that the other witnesses had recognized and reported the object as a UFO, while I hadn't. Apparently, these other witnesses were in some way more attuned to perceiving the UFO, while I had an experience which only barely approached the threshold of my conscious perception.

How many people had seen the Long Beach UFO, and of those, what percentage recognized it as an unknown and furthermore reported it? Perhaps a dozen or two witnesses, at best. Yet, on the other hand, how many more individuals like myself saw but didn't "register" the UFO, and how many forgot or were made to forget the UFO? Possibly hundreds or even thousands? It's impossible to say.

I waited until breakfast the next morning to tell my wife and two daughters the exciting news. They were not skeptical and believed what I told them. In attempting to describe the object, I made a colored drawing using my kids' crayons. This was done soon enough after the actual sightings that I feel it is a fairly accurate, undistorted representation of what I saw. The illustration below is a recreation of this drawing.

While I was excited to think I had seen an actual UFO at close range, I didn't dwell on it.

The following week, I searched the skies for the object whenever I passed the airport and the hospital, yet I saw nothing but the usual airplanes, helicopters, and twinkling stars. Now that I was

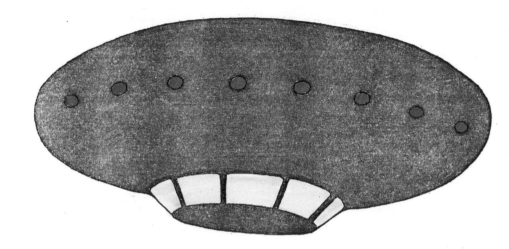

figure 1. THE LONG BEACH UFO - BLIMP
as ~~blimpness~~ it appeared during the first
phase of sightings in mid - February, 1982.
The craft was about 150 feet long and
50 feet high, and was seen at a
distance of approximately 1/4 mile, hovering
about 500 feet in the air.

Earl Heriot's first encounter with the Long Beach Blimp UFO. *Illustration by Earl Heriot, 1983.*

consciously aware of the UFO and prepared to stop and make a detailed observation if possible, the object was nowhere around.

The following Saturday evening on the drive home from a movie, my wife and I decided, on the spur of the moment, to go hunting for the UFO. Twice, we drove past the spot where I had seen the object: first northbound, and then, southbound on the San Diego Freeway. Finding no trace of the UFO, we left the freeway and drove around the airport area on the surface streets, looking for anything out of the ordinary. We spent about a half an hour searching in vain for the UFO. I must admit we were a bit disappointed that the UFO failed to display itself to us.

Incidentally, as this nocturnal saucer hunting episode demonstrates, I had little sense of fear concerning the UFO. I did, however, experience some general paranoia effects during the months that followed. I kept an eye out for the UFO in the weeks that followed, but I was not to see it again.

Perhaps, for reasons known only to the controlling agency or intelligence of the phenomenon, the UFO is initially presented in such a manner that it will be seen and to a degree perceived by a certain percentage of the local population. We can also theorize that perhaps some witnesses are intended to perceive the UFO only on a subconscious, subjective level, while others will have dramatic, conscious sightings and still others will see nothing at all. Then, when enough people have consciously become aware of the UFO's presence through conscious perceptions of the phenomenon, or from news media reports of UFO sightings, the controlling agency prevents further recognition and awareness of the phenomenon by removing the initial stimulus, the traditional UFO image.

During this hypothetical stage of the process, the UFO is either absent, or invisible, if present. The resulting dormant period brings about a cooling off in the public's UFO awareness. With no new reports, the flap seems to have ended. Then, like a wolf in sheep's clothing, the phenomenon reappears, but in a form that makes it easy to dismiss. It imitates an airplane or a helicopter or a blimp, and no one reports it, but witnesses still continue to perceive it on a subconscious level.

Carrying this hypothesis a step further, we can speculate that the UFO agency wants to be perceived at different levels of consciousness, including levels at or under the threshold of conscious awareness. Perhaps the initial sightings and reports of an obvious UFO during any one flap are only a means for preparing us for later phases of UFO perception, wherein we are having subliminal experiences with borderline, chimerical symbols. The ultimate purpose of the phenomenon, of course, remains unknown. If we assume that there is, in fact, some reason or purpose behind the UFO experience, then we can probably safely speculate that some sort of physical, psychological, or spiritual effect is achieved in humans through their response to the UFO image.

Unfortunately, we can't even assume there is any basic purpose to UFO activity. It may very well be meaningless. We may be dealing with the truly absurd and irrational. UFO behavior seems to indicate the functioning of some sort of nonhuman super-intelligence. But I think we are treading on thin ice if we leap to any conclusions beyond that. If UFOs are alien (extraterrestrial or extra-dimensional) in origin, then we cannot expect human reason or purpose from their alien operators.

At any rate, when I next saw the UFO, it was performing a rather inane mimicry of the Goodyear Blimp. As before, I was driving home along the San Diego Freeway at about 6:30 to 6:45 p.m., and was entering Long Beach in the vicinity of the airport. The body of the craft was the same as before: dark, featureless, and football-shaped. But the lighting on it was different. Instead of the row of red circular "running lights," there was a large, rectangular "TV screen" of colored lights about twenty-five feet high and fifty feet long, centrally situated on the main body of the craft. The Goodyear Blimp has a similar sort of electrical reader board, which is used for nighttime displays. The blimp's "screen" consists of thousands of individual light bulbs which flash on and off in a programmed sequence which results in moving words and pictures seen from the ground. This screen is used for advertising purposes.

My UFO, however, displayed only nonsense imagery instead of the normal messages. This visual gibberish consisted of geometric patterns in bright primary colors which transmuted and pulsed in an apparently random and meaningless way. I recall that the patterns themselves were colorful, somewhat hypnotic, and featured diamond shapes which expanded and changed into other shapes and patterns in a constantly shifting display. A drawing of the blimp-UFO with its "TV screen" in operation is shown below.

It occurred to me for a moment that perhaps this was indeed the Goodyear Blimp, and that its control mechanism was on the blink, causing the message it was displaying to be jumbled beyond recognition. If that were the case, however, surely the crew would be aware of the malfunction and would turn off the lights until repairs could be made. I studied the other aspects of the object—the shape of the body, the size of the "gondola" in proportion to the football-shaped main body, and the absence of tail fins. In all details, the object I was seeing did not conform to the Goodyear Blimp as I knew it. The body of the blimp is thinner and more tapered, almost to a point at the tail, whereas the UFO was thicker, with more rounded ends. Even at night, the blimp is clearly silvery in color and reflects ambient light, while my UFO had a dark, non-reflective surface. Another important difference between the blimp and whatever I was seeing is that the gondola of the blimp is quite small, perhaps a sixth the length of the craft, while the gondola of the UFO was quite large and was perhaps a third the length of the craft when observed from the side. Furthermore, the blimp has four tail fins which are visible at night and from some distance, while the UFO had no fins at all.

In the months that followed, I took every opportunity to study the blimp under all kinds of circumstances, including different lighting, angles, and distances. From as far away as a mile or two, the blimp was obviously silvery, and the fins were visible in profile.

While I had previously seen the UFO only in the immediate vicinity of the Long Beach Municipal Airport, I now saw the UFO-disguised-as-blimp at various points along the course of the San Diego Freeway, generally at a distance of about a mile or two ahead of me, all the way from the South Bay Curve on into Long Beach, a

figure 2. THE LONG BEACH UFO - BLIMP
as it appeared during the second phase of sightings
in late Feb., 1982. The craft was identical to
the object witnessed during the first phase sightings,
with the exception of the lighting. The gondola
was unlit and the running lights were no longer
visible, but a "rectangular" "tv screen" approximately 50 x 25 ft
filled the side of the object. This "tv screen"
projected dazzling, brightly colored, geometric patterns
similar to the one shown above.
the author.

The Long Beach Blimp UFO lights up its "TV screen" with wild geometric patterns. *Illustration by Earl Heriot, 1983.*

distance of about twelve miles. At times I caught up with the UFO so that I was practically under it, while at other times it seemed to leap ahead, out-distancing my car. As usual, I was doing fifty to sixty miles per hour in heavy traffic, and had to limit myself to stolen glimpses.

While I had told myself before that if I ever saw the UFO again I would get off the freeway and park for a better view, I wasn't really convinced that this was the UFO, and so once again, I did not stop. Besides, the craft was moving away from me, and I didn't want to risk losing sight of it by stopping. Before I reached the outskirts of Long Beach, I had decided that this probably was my

UFO, and that I was going to follow it for as long as I could. As before, I never really saw it moving; it merely seemed to shift positions between my glances towards it. The thing had an uncanny ability to [Editor: The manuscript has two alternative phrases here that are marked out: "shift around instantly" and "leave me in the dust"] out-distance me whenever I took my eyes off it. I was chasing it at about sixty mph. It would be quite close, say a couple of hundred yards away, when suddenly I'd look up, only to see it a mile or two down the road, about to disappear behind some buildings or hills. I couldn't keep up with the damned thing.

As I entered Long Beach, the UFO, which was some distance away, seemed to be hovering over the airport. I drove another three or four miles until I was past the airport, then took the Lakewood Boulevard off-ramp and headed north. Lakewood Boulevard runs along the eastern edge of the airport, and I thought that perhaps I'd be able to get a better look at the UFO from there. Traffic on this major boulevard averages forty or fifty mph, and is heavy during the evening rush hour, so I still had to limit myself to quick glimpses of the object. I lost track of it for a while, then, as I neared Carson Street, I caught sight of the UFO again, hanging low over the large jet hangar at the McDonnell Douglas Aircraft Plant. It was only a couple blocks ahead of me, on my right, and I momentarily seemed to be gaining on it. Due to the traffic, I still hadn't been able to study the object for longer than a few seconds at a time. I looked up again, and it was suddenly gone, having rapidly shifted position while my eyes were averted.

Cursing the elusive thing, I made a right turn onto Carson Street and immediately caught sight of the UFO again, this time about a mile ahead, very near where I lived at the intersection of Carson Street and Bellflower Boulevard. By the time I reached Bellflower, however, the UFO had rapidly moved off approximately five miles to the south, and appeared to be at a higher altitude, perhaps 1,000 feet, and in the general vicinity of the U.S. Naval Weapons Station in Seal Beach. Being only a few blocks from home, and unable to keep up with the UFO's frog-leaping maneuvers, I gave up the chase and went home. The duration of the episode, from the time I first spotted the UFO at the South Bay Curve to the moment I abandoned the chase in Lakewood, was about a half an hour.

Later that same evening, about 7:30 p.m., I was walking in the parking lot of the Vons Shopping Center at Woodruff Boulevard and Carson Street when I spotted the UFO-blimp again. As before, it was putting on a colorful display of lighted messages on its "TV screen." It appeared to be about five miles away, to the southwest, in the direction of Belmont Shore. While it was too far away to enable me to study the details of the craft itself, the "TV screen" was still clearly visible, as before, generating a seemingly random series of meaningless geometric patterns. I pointed it out to my wife and children and we watched it as we walked toward the supermarket. That was the last time I saw the UFO.

Not long after my initial sightings, perhaps a week or two after hearing my UFO described on Bill Jenkins' *OPEN MIND* show, I wrote out a few pages of rough notes about the sightings, with the idea that I might want to write an account of the incident someday. For some reason, the very existence of these notes began to make me extremely nervous, and I soon put them away in a file folder along with the drawing I had made of the UFO.

In the months that followed, this "nervous" feeling developed into a mild case of paranoia. I had the distinct impression that I was not supposed to tell anyone about what I had seen and, especially, that it would be somehow "dangerous" for me to publish an account of the sightings.

I had read enough UFO literature to know that such paranoia is very common among UFO witnesses, yet it had a firm grip on me and no matter how strongly I reassured myself that my fears were groundless, I couldn't shake the feeling.

I decided the best way to handle it would be to forget about the whole incident, and I therefore turned my attention to other matters.

Then, in May of 1982, as we were packing all our belongings for a move out of state, I was suddenly overcome by paranoia again, even though I hadn't been thinking much about my UFO sightings. Instead of packing the file folder containing my drawing and notes, I impulsively destroyed the papers. I did this without premeditation, on the spot, and I instantly felt better, as if I had been freed of all responsibility in the matter.

Only much later, a full year after the sightings, did I once again begin to think of publishing an account of my UFO experience. I made a few new notes, similar to my original ones, and was relieved to find that my fears had evaporated and I no longer felt any hesitancy to publish the story of my UFO sightings. Either I had outgrown my fears, or it was now "okay" for some reason, and it was no longer necessary for me to remain silent about the Long Beach UFO.

In retrospect, I think it may be significant that I had the UFO experience at the time I did. I had been thinking a great deal about the UFO mystery during the summer and fall of 1982 [Editor: Earl probably means 1981], wrestling with it in my mind. It is such a vastly complex and elusive phenomenon that any attempt to understand it rationally or to learn "the truth about flying saucers" can only result in confusion and frustration. I had been obsessively dwelling on the subject, grappling with it to such a degree that I couldn't get it out of my mind when I went to sleep at night, and often had intense, frightening dreams about UFOs. But these weren't normal nightmares. Rather, they were continuations of the rationalizations which I made during waking hours in my attempts to understand UFOs and thus solve the mystery to my own personal satisfaction.

The focus of these mental struggles were the following basic questions: Do UFOs have any objective reality? If so, what are they? Where are they from? Why are they here?

My meditations on these questions, fueled by all the reading I was doing on the subject, led me down some fascinating paths intellectually, in that I was able to conjecture all sorts of possible answers to the questions, but, interesting as they were, these "solutions" remained mere speculations, and proved nothing about the true nature of UFOs. I remained in the dark on that aspect of the subject.

The final outcome of this process was a decision to neither believe nor disbelieve any particular hypothesis concerning the problems of UFO reality, nature, origin or intent. Much of the literature suggests that UFOs interact with human belief systems, and committing oneself to any particular belief therefore only further obscures the truth by drawing one into the intricacies of the phenomenon in an almost mechanistic way. For instance, if you believe UFOs are hostile and that there is a conspiracy of silence, then you may well be visited by the legendary Men In Black (MIB) who will proceed to harass and intimidate you. Your paranoid beliefs will attract or even create that which you most fear.

When I gave up holding firm beliefs about UFOs, I also stopped trying to understand the phenomenon on a purely rational level. Instead, I decided to withhold judgment, and to continue studying and pondering the phenomenon without becoming too deeply involved emotionally or intellectually. As soon as I took this passive stance two things happened:

1. I was freed from all fear and paranoia effects relating to UFOs, and
2. I suddenly "realized" that UFOs were most likely not understandable, because they are apparently an activity occurring across a wide band of the reality-unreality spectrum; i.e., they are objective and physical (even if only temporarily) and they are subjective and metaphysical, or spiritual.

Rather than clinging to a single solution to the UFO puzzle, it might be more productive to expand our own consciousness by accepting all possible solutions as being equally probable, and even, perhaps, simultaneously true.

While such an outlook has not allowed me to form any firm opinions about what UFOs are or where they are from, it has given me the mental flexibility to continue my study of the problem without any strong negative side effects. When I do still occasionally get "the willies," I just stop thinking or reading about the topic and soon I'm back in balance.

From this perspective, I've been unable to answer any of the basic questions about UFOs which I posed to myself. I still don't know how real they are, what they are, where they're from, or what they're doing here, and particularly, why they're interacting with humans. But I do feel I have a more basic subjective grasp on the phenomenon than I did before, and the UFO experience itself to a great degree was responsible for that.

When you think you've seen something that is not supposed to exist, that, according to all you have been taught, cannot exist, then you have to either relax your belief systems or go mad.

Millions have witnessed UFOs and their belief systems have been forever altered as a result. Why is this happening? I don't think any of us really knows the answer to that question, but we are becoming increasingly aware of the situation. The old, comfortable reality is lost forever.

What I still can't figure out is the purpose behind the funny light show during the second phase of my sightings of the Long Beach UFO. If the UFO was trying to pass for a common blimp, wouldn't a mundane commercial message, real or faked, have been far more convincing and less conspicuous? The razzle-dazzle kaleidoscope of brilliant colors in an absurd TV test pattern almost makes me think the UFO's controllers wanted it to be noticed, that they were trying to get my attention, which they most certainly did. Of course, it's impossible to do more than speculate on events which seem purely irrational to us. All I can say is that I personally perceived the UFO in all of its plumage; whether others noticed it or if it even existed for them at all, I can't say.

While I've said just about all I have to say at this time on the topic of the Long Beach UFO, I somehow feel that this story is incomplete. Something is missing: meaning? There is none that I can determine. An ending? The UFO situation is an open-ended one, and not just for me personally, but for everyone who is concerned with the "UFO problem." The best I can offer you is this two-edged advice: if you think too much about this sort of thing (flying saucers/Forteana/the occult) you'll probably drive yourself half nuts, and if you don't think about it at all, the world will be a far less interesting and wondrous place, and chances are, you'll be missing half of what's going on. My only suggestions are to tread lightly as you walk the fence, to keep your eyes open, stay aware, don't lean too far in any one direction, and try to maintain your mental and spiritual equilibrium. A sense of humor doesn't hurt either. Without it, you run the risk of becoming a fanatic, a cultist, or a crackpot. In other words, yet another victim of the UFO phenomenon.

CHAPTER EIGHT

GRAYS AND CONFUSED

PART ONE: SCIENCE AND GRAYS

s ufology studying physical craft, propulsion systems, and life forms in the sense that we could comprehend any one of these under the light and scrutiny of the scientific method? Some facts can be gleaned with scientific instruments, if not by the method itself. And statistical studies are essential, of course. *The Alien Abduction Files* is an important work by Kathleen Marden and Denise Stoner. My scientific opinion of their abductee study follows: I think that the statistical survey of abductees, including a control group, is sound scientific procedure. The sample size is excellent and the questions are specific enough to give a clear picture of what's going on with the abductee population variation. I think Marden and Stoner present some very clear insights from their research and personal experiences. I do not believe I have ever read before of anyone approaching the abduction experiencers' commonalities in such a controlled scientific manner. I believe that, if for nothing else, this book is groundbreaking in that respect, and I hope that MUFON realizes what Marden and Stoner have done here—fulfilling the MUFON mission statement of "the scientific study of UFOs for the betterment of humanity." When I was in graduate school I was a research assistant to my mentor in human evolution. We were measuring nose shape and how it relates to bioenergetics, how natural selection has favored certain nasal features in specific environments, and how those shapes and volumes relate to calories burned during exercise. We had a sample size of fifty college age adults: twenty-five male and twenty-five female. I have been directly involved in human subject studies and the Marden-Stoner study is as revealing and high quality, scientifically, as what I have done at university.

Is ufology primarily a scientific attempt at understanding? Or does a sense of scientific truth ironically increase faith in our own narratives perhaps too much, beyond even the ecstatic truth? Consider the following points of why ufology is (mostly) unscientific:

1. Ufology is the study of UFOs and related phenomena. UFO means "Unidentified Flying Object." Beginning with "unidentified," the object has immediately become unknown for the very reason it is unidentified. "Flying," then? How can I tell if a UFO is flying, levitating, warping gravity, or just projected like a hologram? Finally, "object." Is a UFO an object, a physical "nuts and bolts" machine? Or is it perhaps a massless hologram? A shadow from another dimension? Careful scrutiny may reveal what the UFO *IS NOT*. But I really do not know what a UFO in fact *IS*.

2. Since I have only ideas of what I am studying in ufology, with correlations in place of proper causations, I can draw no causal relationships, only descriptions of UFO behavior, which I think I understand but have no way of testing. Even the very best, highest quality, most ardently and substantially supported sighting is no more than an anecdote with evidence, scientifically speaking. As mentioned previously, "hard" evidence of UFOs includes radar returns, changes in soil chemistry at reported landing sites, increased background radiation, and electromagnetic anomalies. This is evidence that can be tested with scientific instruments. These instruments are the tools of science, but they are not science itself.

3. Because I do not truly understand or recognize causation in ufology, I must be very careful when making scientific speculations or hypotheses. Science, like any other tool, is intended for a specific purpose. Ufology often pushes the limits of mainstream modern science way past the breaking point. Statistical studies remain, I believe, ufology's most fruitful scientific products.

4. The scientific method is not the only tool of inquiry available, however. There exist religious opinions about UFOs and aliens. Prehistoric cave art begins the recorded human narrative of our discovery and study of "the other side." Some in New Age religions have adopted aliens as their spirit guides and saviors. I remain adamant concerning the use of Herzog's "ecstatic truth" in ufology. I have performed thought experiments that I have referred to as "ufology visions," producing speculative

narratives of UFOs and aliens, while incorporating many opinions and published facts—a proper intellectual setting for "paranormal analysis," as described in my chapter on Grays and ghosts. The tools of science can be put to the UFO question, and can reveal very interesting results. So while I doubt the scientific validity of anything more than a hypothesis in ufology, I do understand very well correlations between sightings and abductions. But correlations are only the very tentative beginning to the use of the scientific method.

5. Ufology is generally pseudoscientific because very few scientists study UFOs! For ufology to become a full-fledged scientific field, many more scientists would have to broaden their scientific worldview. With many researchers in a scientific field comes the opportunity for peer review and the replication of experimental results. I should think that UFOs would be quite interesting to an atmospheric scientist, for example. If ufology were adopted by the scientific community and placed under the combined scrutiny of many researchers, then perhaps we could glimpse the possibility of a future in science for the study of UFOs, and learn more about our planet's anomalous natural behaviors as well.

6. Why have I personally never seen a UFO? I would think that at this point, after studying UFOs for over five years now, I would have seen something. I want to see a satellite make a 90° angle turn and then shoot off into eternity. I desperately want to see something inexplicable! My family and friends have seen UFOs, the strange objects that for some reason I am not meant to see. I am truly frustrated and have tried to attract UFOs psychically. Yes, I really attempt this when I look into a starry sky, as irrational as that might seem. If I use theory of mind on aliens, then I would have to guess they are deliberately hiding their craft from me while showing off for others.

Oliver Sacks' *Hallucinations* mentions ufology cases that are easily explainable by brain chemistry and behaviors. Dr. Sacks asks whether hallucinations are responsible for some paranormal phenomena:

Do the terrifying hallucinations of the night-mare, being ridden and suffocated by a malign presence, play a part in generating our concepts of demons and witches or malignant aliens? Do "ecstatic" seizures...play a part in generating our sense of the divine? Do out-of-body experiences allow the feeling that one can be disembodied? Does the substancelessness of hallucinations encourage a belief in ghosts and spirits?

Sacks is not debunking. As a good scientist he is asking hard questions. Do many UFO researchers hide from hard questions? I don't know the answer, of course, I'm just asking a hard question. If ufology is accepted on faith then it can avoid the hard questions. But if ufology is an investigative enterprise, as daunting as that is, UFO researchers must gather evidence and test it in some manner as described earlier in this book.

"Sleep-paralysising" reduces all alien abductions to a single neurological cause, a natural explanation that is so reductive it excludes most alien abductions. I have experienced sleep paralysis in which I could see the shadows of Grays right outside the sliding doors of my bedroom. I was terrified and could not move. Then I fell back to sleep. Sacks offers an explanation for the effects of cultural background on the hallucinations during sleep paralysis:

> When traditional figures—devils, witches, or hags—are no longer believed in, new ones—aliens, visitations from "a previous life"—take their place.

Sacks includes an incident in which a full-blown abduction experience was triggered by "sleep deprivation and physical exhaustion." The story of this incredible hallucination, experienced during a bike marathon, was told by Michael Shermer in a *Scientific American* column:

> In the wee hours of the morning of August 8, 1983, while I was traveling along a lonely rural highway approaching Haegler, Neb., a large craft with bright lights overtook me and forced me to the side of the road. Alien beings exited the craft and abducted me for ninety minutes, after which time I found myself back on the road with no memory of what transpired in the ship...I was sleepily weaving down the road when my support motor home flashed its high beams and pulled alongside, and my crew entreated me to take a sleep break...Suddenly the members of my support crew were transmogrified into aliens.

Sacks concludes this anecdote:

> After a nap, Shermer recognized this as a hallucination, but at the time it seemed completely real.

This is not an example of debunking, just one anecdote of sleep deprivation and physical exhaustion triggering memories of a science fiction television program complete with fully realistic experiences. This also is not a common example of the alien abduction scenario; in fact, it is atypical of the whole phenomenon. Dr. Oliver Sacks has no interest in debunking UFOs. He is describing the very real and common occurrence of hallucinations in human consciousness. In fact, Sacks displays a profound, almost poetic, mystical evolutionary appreciation for, specifically, the chaotic geometrical patterns seen during migraine episodes:

> Migraine-like patterns, indeed, can be found...in virtually every culture, going back tens of thousands of years...Spontaneous self-organization is not restricted to living systems [like neural networks]; one may see it in the formation of snow crystals, in

the roilings and eddies of turbulent water, in certain oscillating chemical reactions. Here, too, self-organization can produce geometries and patterns in space and time very similar to what one may see in a migraine aura. In this sense, the geometrical hallucinations of migraine allow us to experience in ourselves not only a universal of neural functioning but a universal of nature itself.

To believe that Sacks has motive to debunk UFOs is, frankly, paranoid and petty, and misses the deeper (indeed, "deep time") revelations of neurology that he describes. *Hallucinations* is a marvelous book. Only the most defensive or insincere UFO researcher would deny the very real and common hallucinations that we humans experience naturally. This is not disinformation—it is medical science.

I believe that my own understanding of ufology would greatly increase and deepen if I were to have a UFO sighting. Certainly this is the case with the Grays I have seen in my so-called "hallucinations" and the practical joke that was played on me at 3:30 in the morning by my daughter and close family friends. Reaction to my book *Evolutionary Ufology* has been primarily fear. One friend was not able to make it past the first chapter because she was so disturbed by what I had written. If I were to have a UFO sighting, I am certain my "ufology vision" would expand in scope, probably exponentially. So...

I read *The Short and Simple Practical Guide on How to Summon UFO's* [*sic*] by Jessie A. Contreras, Occult Master Summoner. According to Contreras, I can have a UFO at my beck and call using my willpower and imagination. I tried this long before I read Contreras' guide, and it is good to know that I am not the only one who attempts to contact UFOs with a strong desire or a fervently whispered, "Please, show yourself to me!"

For some reason I doubt the raw strength of my willpower will avail me a glance at one of their shiny ships. Besides, I will never forget what Butch Witkowski recommended when he said that if you ever see a UFO: "Run like hell." Butch, of course, has studied cases of human mutilations by aliens. The cases are nearly identical to cattle mutilations. Forensic study has shown that the victims were alive and aware as they were exsanguinated, genitals removed, anus cored out, and abdomen disemboweled.

Contreras also mentions a "Galactic Federation of Light," which I find fascinating and hopeful.

PART TWO: RELIGION AND GRAYS

The following portion of this narrative would require a book in itself to present the intersection of the Christian religion with the study of ufology. I am not presenting an exhaustive case to you, the reading juror. Instead, what follows is a moment's slice through the Christian religion and ufology phenomenon, the doctrines and worldviews, people's beliefs, and faith. I chose Christian denominations simply because in this predominantly Christian culture, it is much easier to find Christian opinions about UFOs and aliens than it is to find anything by any other religion; in other words, a good starting point—or so I thought. But I very nearly gave up on this portion of the chapter because no one, not even Mormon missionaries, felt comfortable discussing the subject of UFOs and aliens. Through a sleight of guerrilla anthropology I did manage to get a single answer from one of the online Mormon missionaries.

In response to my question, "Are aliens demons?" I very quickly received the response: "Absolutely not!"

But I want to know more of their beliefs on aliens. One stolen secret is not enough!

Lights in the Sky & Little Green Men by Hugh Ross, Kenneth Samples, and Mark Clark is self-proclaimed: *A Rational Christian Look at UFOs and Extraterrestrials.* The book was published by an evangelical creationist denomination and wastes no time leaping from UFOs to demons. The "UFO phenomena [are] counterfeit religious phenomena with direct connection to occultism and probably also the demonic realm," so say the "Christian theologians and apologists" (Ross, Samples, and Clark, 2002).

Hugh Ross vehemently rejects the Extraterrestrial Hypothesis (ETH), based primarily on the belief that aliens are actually demons from Satan and Hell, and that evolution and naturalism are untrue. Ross concludes his point and chapter:

> Life, after all, does exist on Earth; so, where did it come from? It must have come from an intelligence not within but beyond the universe. That, at any rate, is the view of the authors of this book (Ross, Samples, and Clark).

After rejecting evolution, life on other planets, the ETH and the interdimensional hypothesis (IDH), Ross introduces the hypothesis that best fits his religious beliefs, the "Extradimensional Hypothesis," supported by many Bible passages and allowing God that place "beyond the universe." This "EDH" is probably true, even if I already accept the ETH and the IDH. But I was surprised to discover that holding two contradictory or paradoxical beliefs simultaneously is uncommon. I can believe in God and not believe in a god in the same moment. The same goes for my views on aliens and on death.

Brother Michael Dimond pounds on quote after quote with very little analysis, all to prove that UFOs and aliens are demonic in his fifty-four-page booklet *UFOs: Demonic Activity & Elaborate Hoaxes Meant to Deceive Mankind.* Brother Dimond asks:

> If the alleged aliens have super-advanced technology, why would they need to repeatedly perform crude medical experiments on person after person to discover what they need to find out?

I asked the same question in my previous book! Addressing the abduction experience, Brother Dimond declares:

> This experience is not an abduction, but is in reality a visitation by a demon.

I think that if there are demons and Grays, then they must appear and behave damn similar.

"One reason," Dimond declares, "that many people are so interested in UFOs is that they hope for an alien salvation." I agree also with this point, considering that UFOs and aliens are sometimes treated in New Age religions, such as the New Age of Aquarius belief in the "Galactic Federation of Light," as the good guys who supposedly help us in all sorts of loving ways, from assisting in environmental clean-up to "disabling nuclear missiles."

Meanwhile, Dimond makes some "arguments," predictably similar to those found in *Lights in the Sky & Little Green Men*. And he sums up his position on UFOs in no uncertain terms:

> UFOs are simply a massive demonic deception right from the pit of Hell.

Both books are admirable for stating their cases clearly. I doubt very much that either Hugh Ross or Brother Dimond would wish communication with me, a research specialist from MUFON! But I could only enjoy conversation with these men. In many ways my own version of the Grays is a creature nearly identical, in my mind, to a demon "right from the pit of Hell"! Little Green Men or Little Gray Bastards, we're talking about the same thing. And if we're not, then I present that as further proof that demons and Grays are identical in appearance and behavior. The final two words of Brother Dimond's book title, *Deceive Mankind*, is classic Gray behavior. Karla Turner argues that the Grays use deception as a master tool to control people's minds, especially through what she calls "virtual reality scenarios." The Grays—or demons—can make us believe whatever they want.

Contrasting Hugh Ross and Brother Dimond is Barry Downing's opinion— "The God Hypothesis"—that aliens are angelic, from his book *The Bible and Flying Saucers*:

> I believe it is time we explored the possibility that UFOs carry the angels of God. As the Bible says, "Do not neglect to show hospitality to aliens, for thereby some have entertained angels unawares" (Hebrews 13:2) (Downing 1997).

Downing was very clever with his "aliens" and "angels" quote from Hebrews. But many abductees believe exactly that—that aliens really are angels. I am reminded of Karla Turner's book *Masquerade of Angels*. But Downing makes a grand conclusion that aliens assisted in the miracles of Moses and the Israelites. Why? To create a chosen people on a mission from God and to mold their religious development.

Downing makes little mention of Ezekiel's vision of wheels (Ezekiel 1:1-28), but he does comment on the history of ufology claims that cite stories in the Old Testament. A classic treatment on Ezekiel's wheels comes from the interpretations of a former NASA engineer, Josef F. Blumrich, in his book *The Spaceships of Ezekiel*. He meticulously interprets Ezekiel from an engineer's perspective, analyzing line by line and finding evidence of a large spacecraft witnessed by Ezekiel: main underbody of craft is "quasiconical," upper section is the upper half of a sphere, four cylinders descend from the underbody, each with four propellers and its own "crossed wheels," Ezekiel's wheels (Blumrich 1974). Apparently, crossed wheels can roll in any direction; Blumrich finds this particularly interesting. First the craft comes out of the sky, a plasma propulsion system giving a glow to the underside. As the craft approaches the ground, four cylinders fold out from the underbelly. Four propellers on each landing cylinder are then engaged for a soft landing. Finally, the "crossed wheels" allow the craft to move around the surface in any direction.

Blumrich then continues to describe Ezekiel's ride aboard the craft. Straight from Scripture, it sure doesn't sound like Ezekiel was abducted, but he was convinced he was dealing with Angels and the Glory of the Lord. Blumrich, as an engineer, was certain he could understand the story of Ezekiel with a modern ufology- and technology-based interpretation. His scientific analyses were nowhere out of place in a book about the Bible and UFOs! *The Spaceships of Ezekiel* is a fantastic example of scientific thinking directed to ufology.

The Miracle at Fátima (Portugal) on October 13, 1917, is probably the most oft-mentioned religious experience that strongly resembles an encounter with a UFO. After three children in Fátima witnessed a miraculous vision of the Virgin Mary, 70,000 pilgrims arrived and amassed. The enormous crowd witnessed, en masse, the following vision:

> The sun stood out from the rainy sky like a huge silver disk, perceptible to the eye. It began to spin like a wheel of fire, then stop, and rotate again with furious speed, reflecting an array of color that cast its hues upon the crowd and the land below. After three dazzling shows of multi-colored light, the sun suddenly fell from its orbit in a wild zigzag toward the people as if to consume them in fire...Then, amid the terror stricken crowd, the sun did a zigzag path back to the heavens and resumed its natural brilliance (Schulzetenberg 1987).

This very famous close encounter is important to ufology primarily because of the enormous number of witnesses. "Further proof may be found in claims that UFOs are still reported frequently around Fátima today" (Maloney 2011). The Miracle at Fátima is a very important event to Catholicism as well, considered by the Catholic Church to be an actual miracle, a divine vision from God.

Rastafarianism, a Christian denomination that originated in Jamaica and is based primarily on the Book of Revelation, calls for a mass exodus (Old Testament origin?) of all Ethiopia's children to return home. Rastafari believe that Ethiopia is the origin of life itself. This is scientifically possible but, more importantly, Ethiopia is the origin of our species *Homo sapiens*. Also, Ethiopia lies along 45° East Longitude, a possible ley line with effects on human evolution. The line passes between the Black and Caspian Seas, a known refugium for humans during times of dramatic climate change. The religious Rastafarian call for Ethiopia's children to return home might also have roots in ancient knowledge of an actual refugium somewhere in Ethiopia.

In the documentary film *Wake Up* (2010), Jonas Elrod experiences visions of angels, demons, and spirits. Nothing was medically abnormal with his brain. He did not have any form of schizophrenia. Perhaps the most intriguing and chilling moment in the film was a spirit photographed by parapsychologists in Rome, Italy. The image was a face that disturbed Jonas. One of the parapsychologists in the film recognized it, commenting he had seen it many times before, an "alien"—the large teardrop-shaped head with enormous, dark lens-shaped eyes. The face was a Gray. It was positioned directly in front of Jonas when the photo was shot. Jonas also recognized the face. After having considered the film for a week now, I am convinced that Jonas's experiences were the result of serial alien abductions. Though atypical of the alien abduction scenario, the incessant presence of the Gray face in Jonas's life and his ability as well to see orbs suggest previous and ongoing encounters with Gray aliens.

If I could pray, I would pray that my own conclusions are in error. I would pray that the Grays were angels instead of demons. If we are comparing metaphors, demons from Hell or Grays from Zeta Reticuli, then who are the angels? In my previous book I virtually dismissed the idea of friendly space aliens completely. But there may be "friendlies" who manage to survive in the galactic ecology through banding together and cooperating for the good of the whole, some form of Galactic Federation. Was George Adamski at least partially correct with the upbeat nature of his contactee experiences?

PART THREE: DOWN THE RABBIT'S WORMHOLE AND INTO CONFUSION

Perhaps some contactees or experiencers really have been in contact with representatives of a Galactic Federation, similar to that "imagined" by Carl Sagan in his novel *Contact*. These aliens may be interested in the possibility of the human race joining the Federation, but not before we beat the final variable of the Drake Equation: survive this stage of destructive technological culture or go extinct. We must prove that we are not a dangerous, self-destructive, short-sighted, closed-minded, xenophobic, violent, and actively warring hominid species. Failing that, and without the combined protection of a benign Federation, Earth will forever belong to the galactic apex predators, the Grays and their competitors. We must first forward our own Federation or all is lost.

How can we ever know the "good" or "evil," assistance or hindrance, kindness or utility, and reality or unreality? Grays use virtual-reality scenarios to deceive individuals, usually accompanying abduction and experimental medical procedures. Then they wipe the victim's memory. David Barker once suggested that everyone has been or is being abducted, and only the individuals who have some memory of the experience are called "abductees." We may all be abductees! Mr. Krister proposed the possibility of missing time measured, not in minutes, hours or days, but in weeks, months or years—perhaps even decades. To carry this off would require amazing cooperation and coordination among the hive-like Grays, and I find it a totally credible speculation. If "massive missing time" is possible and true, coupled with a worldwide virtual-reality scenario, then it becomes quickly impossible to know for certain which memories are trustworthy and which have been compromised, as well as just how much missing time has actually passed. So then, when the hell are we?

Many folks in ufology refer to questions like the above as "going down the rabbit hole," and of course it is. But the questions are there, they do have meaning, and they are relevant to an understanding of UFOs. What is a UFO? Where do UFOs come from? Why are they here? Who controls UFOs? These are just the first tentative questions. If I were to skip further down the list of inquiry, I would eventually come to questions like the following. Have I been abducted? What are the Grays? What do they want? What is the purpose of abductions and mutilations? Later, the questions become so bizarre that my mind trips over them. I strongly believe the majority of confusion comes from the Grays themselves.

CHAPTER NINE

I was intrigued by one of the events Earl briefly mentions in his working notes and that is the "Men In Plaid" episode that occurred in the spring of 1983 while he was writing the Long Beach section of his narrative. I asked Earl if he has a current memory of these events. He says he recalls only one puzzling incident involving so-called "Men In Plaid." He had taken his daughters to the city library where they checked out a humorous children's book about aliens coming to Earth. Earl noticed that the book's illustrations featured fat humanoid aliens dressed in plaid suits and he made a mental connection between these "Men In Plaid" and the traditional "Men In Black" or MIBs of ufological lore who are said to harass UFO witnesses into maintaining secrecy about what they've seen. He doesn't remember the title of the book, but thinks it may have been the very popular *Fat Men from Space* by Daniel Pinkwater, which was first published in 1976 and has since been reprinted many times. After glancing at the book in the library, he didn't give the idea of "Men In Plaid" any further thought. However, a few days later, while on a coffee break in the cafeteria at the building where he worked, he spotted a pair of unusual looking men in the checkout line. They were holding coffee and pastries and conversing with one another.

Earl states that:

They looked completely out of place there, and I got the impression they were foreigners visiting here who were totally unfamiliar with our American culture. They spoke a broken sort of English, and had thick accents, but I couldn't say what nationality they might have been. Perhaps something European. What really struck me as odd is that both men were quite overweight, and both were dressed in plaid from head to foot, with plaid pants and plaid suit coats. When they got to the cashier and it was time to pay, they became utterly confused. They had plenty of money on them but didn't seem to understand our currency system, and were unable to figure out what to give the cashier. It was only with her help that they settled their bill. I remember thinking at the time that it was an example of synchronicity that I encountered real life "Men In Plaid" who behaved in a way you might expect aliens in disguise to behave, a short time after coming across the fictional idea of such beings in a book written for children. While there was nothing about the incident that directly related to UFOs, this did happen about the same time that I was writing my account of the Long Beach sightings.

"I do wonder," he speculates, "if these strange beings weren't sent to pressure me into keeping quiet about my experiences in Long Beach by reminding me, in a whimsical sort of way, about the more sinister MIBs who have threatened many other UFO witnesses, if you believe those stories."

I asked Earl if he had any opinions about the possible meaning or purpose of the strange events he experienced in 1981 and 1982.

In your typical UFO abduction story, the witness usually comes away from the event with some kind of message, a set of ideas or a philosophy that the aliens have communicated to the abductee, either through direct speech or by mental telepathy. And maybe if I agreed to be hypnotized and was made to relive the experience, I would report something similar. Maybe under hypnosis I would report that the aliens had told me I was special, a chosen one they had selected to convey to all mankind an important idea: that we are all one, God's children, or that humans are destroying the planet through our misuse of Earth's natural resources. Maybe it would be a religious or metaphysical message, or a dire warning of impending natural disaster, ecological collapse, a third world war that reduces Earth to a smoldering ruin—you name it.

In the working notes for Earl Heriot's written account of the Long Beach Blimp UFO incident, he briefly mentions a few sightings of unusual aerial objects that occurred after his return to Oregon in 1982. The first of these sightings dates to June of 1983. All he wrote in his notes about this event was the phrase, "Red cigar-shaped cloud—disappears." Apparently he had planned to discuss this sighting in more detail in his narrative but never got around to it. I asked Earl if he remembers anything about it.

> Only a little. At the time it happened we were living on Fourth Street in Salem. When we moved back to Oregon in 1982, the first place we lived in was a rental home on Market Street. We didn't stay there for long, a year or less, and then we moved to another rental house on Fourth Street. This is where I saw the red cigar-shaped cloud.

At the end of the note about the cigar-shaped cloud, Earl mentions another unusual sighting that presumably also occurred in 1983. That part of the note reads: "August/September? Flock of white glowing silent doves in perfect V-formation."

Another odd sighting listed in his working notes is described in more detail. The note for it reads: "May 1984: Orange/red glowing object—meandering slowly, aimlessly. Bright—no running lights. 5 miles away. Disappeared after a couple minutes."

Earl remembers the "orange/red glowing object" in some detail.

> At that same house on Fourth Street where I had seen the cigar-shaped object, I saw what I thought was maybe ball lightning moving through the sky. The object glowed like it was red hot. It was spherical and it rolled through the air just like a bowling ball. I saw it from my backyard late one afternoon. I can still picture it. It was a couple miles away and was fairly large, maybe about the size of a car. It glowed bright red and its surface was bubbly, like the material was boiling. The thing rolled through the sky in a horizontal line. From my perspective, it was just above the treetops and power lines. It didn't take long for it to cross my field of vision and then it was gone. I thought it might have been ball lightning, but it's not like the weather was stormy that day—it wasn't. Maybe it was some kind of weird alien craft.

These incidents suggest that while Earl had left Long Beach behind, the UFO phenomenon had not finished with him. He was still seeing strange things in the sky that he could not explain away as mundane phenomena, and they made enough of an impression on him to make him want to write about them later, even though ultimately he did not document them in any detail beyond the fleeting mention of these objects in his working notes.

CHAPTER TEN

WHEN GRAYS ATTACK

G rays are not solely interested in us for reproductive experimentation and hybridization. They also have a history of attacking and killing humans, a history that proves the aliens are not and never have been our friends but our enemy masters. Sometimes the attacks are deliberate and sometimes people just get in the way, like a human unaware of the ants it is stepping on. This chapter covers primarily the deliberate alien attacks, but also those Close Encounters of the Sixth Kind that were ultimately but not intentionally fatal. I also include alien abductions, because Close Encounters of the Fourth Kind can lead to the Sixth Kind during an abduction (e.g. raping human subjects causes physical, mental, and emotional injury).

CLOSE ENCOUNTERS OF THE SIXTH KIND: INJURY OR DEATH CAUSED BY A UFO. (SEE GLOSSARY.)

This is not a popular view in ufology, that the aliens torture and kill humans; nevertheless, it is a fact of the Grays' incessant presence that they are violent psychopaths. Folks want adorable E.T., and who can blame them? People are scared animals. So scared, that alien attacks are rarely and scarcely covered in the literature. I am especially indebted in this chapter to the excellent book *Close Encounters of the Fatal Kind* by Nick Redfern. Redfern has placed the scarier side of aliens and UFOs in one convenient tome, a classic on alien attacks. I also found much information in Mack Maloney's *UFOs in Wartime*, an excellent book of truly incredible encounters not often mentioned in ufology. And there are more cases out there, some of them perhaps older and overlooked. People want to believe so much in the benevolent space brother scenario that ufology has waxed on and off, even in light of cases like Captain Mantell, who was pursued in 1948 by a UFO and died in a subsequent crash. But the truth of the little Gray bastards has never budged.

Chet Dembeck states in his *We Are Not Alone and They Are Not Our Friends*:

> If there is one misguided theme I have heard repeated many times in and outside of the UFO community, it is the notion that UFOs and extraterrestrials are our benevolent technological and spiritual superiors who are only trying to watch over us and gently guide humankind from a path of nuclear self-destruction.

Nick Redfern finishes his excellent book *Close Encounters of the Fatal Kind* with a serious caution on the last page:

> To UFO witnesses, investigators, abductees, researchers, and just about anyone and everyone thinking of immersing themselves in the world of the flying saucer, I say this: tread very carefully, lest you tread no more. Ever.

Or, as mentioned earlier, Butch Witkowski is famous for saying that if you see a UFO, "Run like hell."

And I say that Dembeck, Redfern, and Witkowski are absolutely correct, which means it's too late for everyone involved with this book, including you, dear reader. In *Evolutionary Ufology* I suggested possibly using a handgun on a Gray to kill it; I retract that suggestion here. They know about guns. Your primitive hand-held gas-propelled projectile launcher is worse than useless

TIMELINE OF ALIEN ATTACKS

1886
UFO IRRADIATES FAMILY OF NINE IN VENEZUELA.

1914
THE "ANGELS OF MONS."

1932
LINDBERGH BABY IS ABDUCTED FROM HOME IN EAST AMWELL, NEW JERSEY.

1937
AMELIA EARHART VANISHES OVER THE PACIFIC.

against the Grays—they could use it against you, like make a screen image out of someone you love so you shoot them instead. Or convince you psychically to shoot yourself. Despite what Phil Schneider (who lectured about government involvement with ufology topics and was then found dead, some think murdered) claimed, I do not believe our handguns can protect us, less more kill a Gray.

Below is a timeline of major known Gray attacks on humans, followed by varied information about some of the events.

So many times, repeated with parrot-like squawks, the history of UFOs and flying saucers is said to have begun with Kenneth Arnold's sighting in 1947 of—STOP! We all know the tale, for christsakes! My next ufology book should be titled *Kenneth Arnold Is Not In This Book*. What follows is just as much a break from the repetitive, for even the popular cases are considered from the perspective that the aliens only hurt us—that's all we ever get out of the deal. That is why I do not believe in the Greada Treaty signed by Eisenhower. There is only one treaty: we, the conquered, are at the mercilessness of the Grays.

The timeline above and the analyses to follow cover only the last 130 years of alien attacks on humans, and most of those attacks occurred after the 1940s (e.g. 1967 was a year with four attacks). This is, partially, an artifact of what is known as "the pull of the recent." In other words, the closer to present day in our timeline, the more incidents we see. The main reason for this is that older accounts of Gray attacks simply were not recorded, and if they were, then they were lost to time. But evidence exists that supports the speculation that aliens have been our predators for millions of years. For the purpose of this chapter, however, the last 130 years should suffice to scare you enough for the next several pages and probably the next several days.

1886

On the night of October 24, 1886, a family of nine in a small Venezuelan village were irradiated by something that emitted "a loud humming noise and a vivid, dazzling light" with no associated heat. The family immediately grew very ill:

〉〉〉

1942
THE BATTLE OF LOS ANGELES.

1943
SILVER DISKS ATTACK B-17 OVER STUTTGART.

1944
NAVY PATROL PLANE DISAPPEARS AFTER ENCOUNTERING BRIGHT ORB.

1945
UFOS MORPH INTO TENTACLES AND WRAP AROUND AIRCRAFT CARRIER.

vomiting, swellings (especially in the face), then "large black blotches" that later peeled off and became "raw sores," and hair loss on the irradiated side of the body (Dembeck 2012).

This late nineteenth-century case, in my opinion, can only be explained by the UFO. Only very bright light was reported, but the family was inside their hut. They saw the light but not its source. What device with a humming noise and bright lights could possibly have irradiated nine people in 1886? A natural event, perhaps? But I offer no "swamp-gassing" or "weather-ballooning" alternatives to posit. No radioactive weapons or devices of any kind existed to irradiate this Venezuelan family 130 years ago—no human weapons.

But the Grays have had beam weapons for probably millions of years. Why would the Grays irradiate nine people? An experiment? I am inclined to conclude that this case was not an intentional attack. More likely, the family's hut was just in the wrong place when a UFO vented radiation and then took off. Nevertheless, there is a callous thoughtlessness here. The Grays who irradiated the Venezuelan family 130 years ago did not even know enough to care, or did not care enough to know. Either way, this is a case of the Grays acting with malice, even if it was unintentional.

1914

The Battle of Mons, beginning August 1914, set up 80,000 British soldiers against a German force of twice that number (Maloney 2011). The army that came to the assistance of the British was wholly otherworldly:

> The story went that just as the Germans were about to crush the British force at Mons, to the astonishment of both sides, an army of ghostly archers appeared. These bowmen fired their arrows at the Germans, cutting down enough of them that the overwhelmed British army was able to declare victory. It was even said that many of the German soldiers killed during the battle had died of arrow wounds (Maloney).

Setting aside for the moment the possibility that ghostly archers actually did assist the British in their victory, what were these reinforcements? The first

TIMELINE OF ALIEN ATTACKS CONTINUED . . .

1946
BRAZILIAN MAN HIT BY ALIEN BEAM AND MELTS INTO CHUNKS.

1947
UFO KILLS DOG WITH FALLING SLAG IN MAURY ISLAND, TACOMA, WASHINGTON.

1948
CAPTAIN THOMAS MANTELL JR. SHOT DOWN BY GIANT UFO.

answer is the Grays. Why did they interfere with a battle in World War I? Probably to feel the thrill of killing. Assisting the British, unless it served some larger Gray purpose, was not the aliens' intention at all. Why did the soldiers see ghostly archers? The Grays adopted a screen image from the collective unconscious of the British soldiers and showed them what they most wanted to see: a force of angels descending from heaven to smite their evil enemy; i.e., the British were convinced by the Grays that God was on their side. This religious conviction alone might have been enough to turn the battle in favor of the outnumbered British army. And what of all the Germans the Grays killed that day? Germany is now, of course, an ally to the United States. The Grays are not.

1942

In the early hours of February 25, 1942, a giant object hung in the skies above Los Angeles and was witnessed by a million people. Army anti-aircraft guns fired on the object for sixty-eight minutes, but nothing affected it. Finally, the object moved off south-west and disappeared from view of the glaring searchlight beams. Six people died indirectly in the "Battle of Los Angeles" (Maloney 2011).

How is this incident an "attack," let alone a "battle"? The giant object did not react in a hostile manner, except to allow the Army to waste its ammunition on it for eight minutes more than an hour. Falling shell fragments did injure, but not kill, two people. Many more people were terrified. But no one thought the large object might be an alien craft. Everyone was convinced the object was a Japanese balloon or perhaps airplanes. But the object was one single object (possibly with a 300-foot diameter), and it moved far too slowly for an aircraft. It was not a balloon, because there is no balloon on Earth, then or now, that can take sixty-eight minutes of continuous anti-aircraft fire and then just float away (Maloney).

The lives of those who died and those who were injured in the Battle of Los Angeles count. If the giant object had not inexplicably hung around for an hour and eight minutes, then no one would have died as a result of the object's existence. In other words, this "battle" is another example of thoughtless, callous Gray behavior.

I do not, however, believe that thoughtlessness explains this incident. The aliens monitored World War II, using Foo Fighter orbs to follow aircraft. They knew that the United States was at war with the Axis powers and the Japanese Empire. The Grays, therefore, also knew that incursion into sensitive airspace over Los Angeles would terrify the humans on the ground, and prove the anti-aircraft ineffectual. Or maybe they didn't predict anything at all. The Battle of Los Angeles is a good example of the Grays intruding where they shouldn't and resulting in people hurt and killed.

1943

In a massive air battle over Stuttgart, Germany, on September 6, 1943, "some witnesses thought they saw some…mysterious [silver] disks land on the wing of one B-17 and start it burning" (Maloney 2011).

The silver disks were like mini-UFOs, each about the size of a silver half-dollar. The size indicates some form of remotely operated weapon. The real mystery, however, is why the disks destroyed an Allied B-17 but not any Nazi targets. This incident does support my continued contention that the aliens have much in common with Nazi mentality and behavior.

1944

In June of 1944, a United States Navy patrol plane crashed into the Pacific after an encounter with a bright sphere. The patrol plane was never found (Maloney 2011). And I suspect something similar occurred to Amelia Earhart.

A year after the patrol plane's disappearance, an incredibly bizarre encounter occurred to a United States aircraft carrier in the Pacific. The radar operator saw a huge mass of plots, what looked like upwards of 300 separate incoming bogies. But then the mass of plots merged and began to take shape on the radar screen—they transformed into giant "tentacles" that wrapped themselves around the carrier! The mysterious radar return vanished when planes reached its point of origin (Maloney).

TIMELINE OF ALIEN ATTACKS CONTINUED . . .

APRIL 1959

UFOLOGIST MORRIS K. JESSUP "SUICIDED."

1961

THE BETTY AND BARNEY HILL ABDUCTION.

1963

PRESIDENT JOHN F. KENNEDY ASSASSINATED.

MARCH 1967

CUBAN MIG EXPLODES AFTER WEAPONS LOCK ON UFO.

1946

On the evening of March 4, 1946, a Brazilian farmer named João Prestes Filho was shot by a bright, hot beam from an unseen object in the sky above his village. He was severely burned instantaneously and screamed for help. On his way to the hospital, Filho's body began decomposing. The man "melted away in gooey chunks" (Redfern 2014) until he finally died after hours of agony. But why?

One common man, middle-aged, hard-working, and killed for no reason. I reject any notion that the beam that killed Filho so horribly was in any way native to this planet; this was no secret military weapons test, and certainly not an aberrant weather phenomenon. The case appears to be what it is: a directed beam attack on Filho, solely out of randomly placed malice by the Gray aliens. The results of the beam attack are almost too horrible to contemplate, and prove further the mad sadism of the Grays.

1947

The Maury Island incident, beginning June 21, 1947, is well-known in ufology. Harold Dahl was on his salvage boat with his son, hired hands, and the Dahls' dog. A flotilla of donut-shaped UFOs flew in formation over Puget Sound in Tacoma, Washington. One of the six torus-shaped UFOs was wobbling at a lower altitude and dropping white-hot metal from the hole of the donut. Other craft dropped altitude and nudged the failing UFO into a controlled flight path. That path crossed directly over the Dahls' boat. Falling hot metal slag damaged the boat, injured Harold Dahl's son, and killed the family dog (Maloney 2011).

The tale continues with Men In Black and deaths assumed associated with the Maury Island incident. Supposedly, the military gathered up the slag, put some of it on a cargo plane, and took off for Wright Field, Ohio. But the Boeing B-29 never made it. The plane "burst into flames, plunged to the ground, and killed [Lieutenant Frank Mercer Brown and Captain William Lee Davidson] in a fiery explosion near Kelso, Washington" (Maloney).

So, in total, how many people died as a direct, causal result of the UFO slag? Zero evidence exists that the slag on board Lieutenant Brown and Captain Davidson's B-29 caused the accident that led the plane to explode. How would

》》》

JUNE 1967

UFOLOGIST FRANK EDWARDS DIES FROM AN APPARENT HEART ATTACK.

JULY 1967

UFO ACTIVATES NUCLEAR MISSILE "LAUNCH IN PROGRESS" AT MINOT AIR FORCE BASE, NORTH DAKOTA.

SEPTEMBER 1967

SNIPPY THE HORSE IS THE FIRST CONFIRMED VICTIM OF THE ANIMAL MUTILATION PHENOMENON.

this occur? Did the metal suddenly change its material properties? Further, what kind of metal was the slag, anyway? Was any sample ever collected and tested? Since I have no answers, I cannot evaluate the possible lethality of the collected slag. I simply cannot find a causal relationship between the slag and the explosion of the B-29.

I have always felt this way about the Maury Island incident: the one and only truly direct fatal victim of the slag-dropping UFO was the Dahl family dog. Where on the body did the slag hit the dog? What breed was the dog? Was it male or female? But, most importantly, what was the name of the Dahls' family dog? I am not making light of the incident here. I am damn serious. The one definite victim of the Maury Island incident and I cannot discover anything at all about the Dahl dog. Further, was the dog buried at home or did Harold Dahl give his dog a burial at sea?

We know the name of the canid cosmonaut Laika. So why can't I find the name of the dog killed by a UFO?

I believe that many of the questions concerning this classic case could come to light if research focused on some of the unknowns mentioned above. The incident has become mired in conspiracy theories that reach much further than a close encounter with a failing UFO. Find a sample of the Dahl slag and test it for metals analysis. Find anything at all about the Dahls' dog, starting with its name; a photo would be nice, too. The true mystery of the Maury Island incident is the dead dog.

1948

Captain Thomas Mantell, pilot in the United States Air Force, was killed by a giant UFO on January 7, 1948, over Kentucky (Dembeck 2012 and Redfern 2014). Mantell climbed to 25,000 feet in his P51 Mustang. The UFO fired a beam weapon at him and the plane dropped to the ground. However, after a drop of around 25,000 feet, "each and every one of [Mantell's] bones were utterly shattered, [but] there was not even a cut or a scratch on Mantell's skin" (Redfern). Further, Mantell's P51 "was not at all badly damaged—although the wings had broken off the aircraft on impact" (Redfern). The punchline is

TIMELINE OF ALIEN ATTACKS CONTINUED . . .

1968
UFO INCINERATES NORTH VIETNAMESE SOLDIERS.

1975
UFO "ZAPS" TRAVIS WALTON.

1976
JONATHAN LOUETTE MUTILATION CASE.

1977
"CHUPA-CHUPAS" ATTACK VILLAGERS IN COLARES, BRAZIL.

the official story that Captain Mantell, an experienced fighter pilot, was erroneously chasing either a weather balloon or Venus ("Venusing"?).

Climbing to 15,000 feet, Mantell saw the UFO and radioed to the tower, "It appears to be a metallic object…and it is of tremendous size…I'm still climbing…I'm trying to close in for a better look…It's above me and I'm gaining on it. I'm going to 20,000 feet." And then his final words, "My God, I see people in this thing!" Mantell's P-51 Mustang fell from 25,000 feet and "belly-flopped" on the ground with much less force than gravity dictates (Redfern).

The attack on Captain Mantell was an unnecessary and unmeasured reaction to such little provocation. Mantell did pursue the UFO, but his P51 Mustang was a single propeller fighter and the cockpit did not even have an oxygen supply. What kind of threat was Mantell to the UFO? None at all, of course. But the UFO fired a beam weapon anyway, killing Captain Mantell in the process. So naturally the question, "Why?"

The Grays certainly sent a message: "Pursue us with your flying machine. Watch as we drop it from the sky with anti-gravity grace. Marvel at the state of the pilot, not a scratch on him yet all his bones shattered. Look at your fighter plane, broken and futile against us." It is an alien message with the oft-repeated theme of their technological superiority.

1951

In the spring of 1951, United States Army Private Francis Wall's company was fighting in North Korea. Suddenly, an orange glowing UFO appeared. It changed color to a blue-green, and began pulsating. Wall fired at it from his bunker, but to no effect. The UFO then swept Wall's unit with a heat ray, as Wall recalls: "We were attacked…We were swept by some form of ray. It was like a searchlight. You would feel a burning, tingling sensation all over your body [when it hit you], as though something were penetrating you" (Maloney 2011). After firing its ray, the UFO shot up into the sky and was gone.

In times of conflict, the Grays sometimes attack one side and not the other. Are they experimenting with human war by intervening on behalf of a chosen side? Is it mere sport? One thing is certain about the Gray intentions—they are reveling in human pain, and wars are the penultimate expression of human pain on a massive scale.

〉〉〉

1978
AUSTRALIAN PILOT DISAPPEARS DURING UFO ENCOUNTER.

1979
"FIRST" HUMAN MUTILATION CASE.

1979
FIREFIGHT AT DULCE BASE, NEW MEXICO.

1980
BETTY CASH RECEIVES FATAL DOSE OF RADIATION FROM UFO.

1953

November 23, 1953: air traffic controllers detected a UFO on radar near Lake Superior. An F-89 was scrambled to intercept. On board: the pilot Lieutenant Felix Moncla and radar operator Lieutenant Robert Wilson. The F-89 chased the UFO for half an hour before finally catching up with it over Lake Superior. The air traffic controllers watched the screen as the UFO blip merged with the F-89 blip, and then only the UFO blip remained. It accelerated and disappeared from radar. The operators tried to contact the F-89, but it had vanished, and no remains were ever found (Maloney 2011).

Were Lieutenants Moncla and Wilson blasted from the sky in their F-89? Or did the UFO truly "consume" the jet and its occupants? It is possible that the jet was not destroyed at all, but taken on board the UFO. If so, Moncla and Wilson are two abductees who were never returned.

1956

Early on July 22, 1956, United States Air Force pilot Major Mervin Stenvers was flying a C-131 cargo plane from Hamilton Air Force Base, California, to Albuquerque, New Mexico. The C-131 was at 15,000 feet when it was attacked by a flying saucer. The craft apparently collided with the C-131, which fell from the sky. Major Stenvers skillfully gained control of the cargo plane and set down safely in Bakersfield, California. The flying saucer had destroyed the tail section of the plane (Maloney 2011). Stenvers was one hell of a pilot!

Even if this incident represents an accidental midair collision with a UFO, the Gray pilots of the craft simply are not that incompetent. If they crashed their flying saucer into the plane's tail, then that is precisely what they intended to do. Stenvers' piloting must have given them some unhuman delight.

1959

On the night of February 1 and early hours of the second, 1959, nine Russian hikers encountered an alien force that drove them mad with fear and ultimately killed them on the slopes of Otorten Mountain, also known as "Dead Mountain," in the Russian Ural Mountains (Eichar 2013).

TIMELINE OF ALIEN ATTACKS

1982
UFO ACTIVATES SEVERAL NUCLEAR MISSILES IN THE SOVIET UNION.

1993
UFOLOGIST RON RUMMEL "SUICIDED" IN PORTLAND, OREGON.

1996
PHIL SCHNEIDER "SUICIDED."

2003
TODD SEES ALIEN MURDER CASE.

Donnie Eichar's book *Dead Mountain: The Untold True Story of the Dyatlov Pass Incident* is meticulously well researched and offers answers to the causes of madness and death. However, Eichar takes a decidedly anti-ufology stance from the very beginning of his book. He calls UFO and alien speculation "crackpot" and offers this explanation why:

> 7. SPACE ALIENS, ETC. There were, of course, those who would put forth interstellar visitation as the answer to Sherlock Holmes's "whatever remains, however improbable." But I was holding out hope that I could find an explanation that didn't involve extraterrestrials. I'm not saying I don't entertain the idea of life existing out there somewhere in the vast universe, but if one is going to fall back on malevolent alien visitors without backing it up with evidence, one may as well throw ghosts, the hand of God, and devious subterranean gnomes into the mix. Aliens were off the table (Eichar).

Eichar flat out denies any evidence for UFOs, yet presents several pieces of evidence that actually support the alien speculation! One of two hiking groups, who had been present on Otorten Mountain the night of the incident, reported having seen a "light [that] was so bright that even those hikers who were preparing to sleep in tents went out to look at it. For some time, the sound of strong thunder came from afar" (Eichar). Other hikers had seen "fire orbs" in the direction of Otorten Mountain in early February 1959. Nikolay Kuzminov wrote that he thought the deaths of the nine hikers was caused by "fire orbs" (Eichar).

Lead Investigator Lev Ivanov, a proponent of the "fire orb" explanation, said the following in 1990:

> I can't tell for sure whether those orbs were weapons or not, but I'm certain that they were directly related to the death of the hikers....Someone wanted to intimidate people or show off power, and so they did so by killing [the] hikers. I know all details of this event and can say that only those who were inside the orbs know more than me. Whether there were "people" inside that time or any time is yet unclear.

Ivanov referred to the orbs more generally as "energy bundles unexplained by modern science" and their attack as using an "unknown compelling force" (Eichar). He concludes that, "I had a clear idea of the sequence of [the nine hikers'] deaths from a thorough examination of their bodies, clothes and other data. Only the sky and its contents—with unknown energy beyond human understanding—were left out" (Eichar).

Others saw orbs and strange lights on Otorten in February. A group of search volunteers witnessed a "strange celestial phenomenon" early February 17. Vladislav Karelin and friend Georgy Atmanaki "saw a large light spot [that] grew larger. A small star appeared in its center and also grew bigger." Others saw "a slow-moving orb that 'pulsed' in the sky…" Further, a "group of hikers from the geographical faculty was at Chistop Mountain and (according to the witnesses) they saw some fire orbs on the same days, in the first days of February in the direction of Otorten Mountain. The same fire orbs were noticed later as well. Why is that? Could they have caused the death of the group?"

Finally, "a new piece of evidence emerged that would only bolster the theories of those who felt the orbs had something to do with the fate of the Dyatlov group. That evidence was in the final photographs taken by the hikers before they died" (Eichar); specifically, the final frame of film in Georgy Krivonishchenko's camera that shows a bright rectangular lens flare, possibly a shot of the alien orbs that drove the Dyatlov group mad with fear, scared enough to flee their tent in the dark and cold, wearing only underclothes and no shoes.

Despite all of the evidence supporting an alien attack, Eichar concludes that twin vortices formed on either side of the tent the night of February 1, 1959, and produced sound louder than a roaring locomotive, as well as infrasound. Eichar "swamp-gasses" an answer to the Dyatlov question in naturally occurring vortices and infrasound. Infrasound, generated by the high speed vorticular winds, caused anxiety and, ultimately, irrational panic. Terrified and confused, the hikers knifed open their own tent from the inside, then fled into the night where they died of hypothermia.

But Eichar's book contains more support for the "fire orb" hypothesis than it does for his naturally occurring vortices and infrasound. In other words, nine Russian hikers were killed by Grays on the night of February 1 and early second, 1959.

The Grays took form as orbs, entered the hikers' tent, and transformed back to Grays. The young hikers were terrified and before the Grays could paralyze them they had escaped the tent in their bare feet and underclothes. The nine hikers, split into three groups, soon became hypothermic and their paths confused. Then the Grays hunted them down and shot them dead with a gravity beam weapon (Ivanov's "unknown compelling force") that "sunburned" their skin and submitted the internal organs and skeleton to forces strong enough to crush their insides. Following the pointless murders, the Grays re-formed into orbs and were not seen again on the mountain until February 17 by Karelin and Atmanaki. The question "Why?" is answered by the act itself: murder.

Speaking of murder, some ufologists who have been killed—ultimately, by the aliens—were "suicided": either murder made to look like suicide or murder by inducing suicide.

Ufologist Morris K. Jessup, author of the classic *The Case for the UFO*, was found asphyxiated by carbon monoxide poisoning in his car on April 20, 1959. His death appears to be a bit of both "suicides." First, murder by inducing suicide, and then murder by assisting suicide. Jessup was in a deep depression following his divorce and rebuke from his university for studying UFOs. Ufologist Richard Ogden believes that Jessup was fed detailed information on how to go about offing himself at a time when Jessup was seriously considering suicide (Sprague 2014).

All that we know for sure is that a man named Morris K. Jessup wrote a book about UFOs. His life began to suffer afterwards. His university did not take him as seriously and pulled funding from research (Sprague). His wife divorced him. He became severely depressed. He wrote about killing himself (Sprague). Then he was found dead of carbon monoxide poisoning. A sad man with a sad life and a sad death. If this is what can happen to a person after writing one UFO book, then how about those who write two or more? And just what was it that Jessup said in his book that so upset his Gray editors to the point of "suiciding" this sad man?

1961

"Suiciding" is a tenuous conclusion because it is hard to support; but it is an attack, so it is included here. Alien abductions are also herein considered as a Gray attack.

Beginning with the Betty and Barney Hill abduction on September 19, 1961, alien abductions rose to the level where the public was finally aware of the phenomenon. Further, anyone who doubts that abduction is an attack needs to hear the horrifying hypnotic regression audio of Barney Hill as he relives his rape by the Grays. Since the popularization of the Hill abduction case, millions of other people have realized the reality of their own abductions. So this incident must extend beyond 1961 to the present day, and also into lesser-known and unknown previous alien abductions stretching back millions of years. Probably billions of people have been abducted over the past eight million years. Alien abduction, whatever the purpose of the ends, is rape, mutilation, and murder by the means.

1967

In March of 1967, Cuban air defense tracked a UFO approaching the coastline from the northeast (Redfern 2014). Two MiG-21 fighters took off in pursuit of what was described as a craft "circular in shape, and highly reflective" (Redfern). The first fighter got a radar weapons lock on the UFO when suddenly the plane just disintegrated. The UFO shot straight up to 100,000 feet and then headed for South America (Redfern).

This is an astonishing case, harkening back to Captain Mantell. The weapon used by the Grays sounds similar in effect to both the Mantell case and the "unknown compelling force" that killed the Dyatlov Pass victims. I have speculated that the weapon used in all three of these cases was some form of gravity beam, and I realize just how speculative that sounds. Yet, a beam weapon with the properties of controlled gravity does explain the reported attacks.

Perhaps the most astonishing fact about this case is that the Cubans did not overreact. They pursued and attempted to destroy an unknown invader in their airspace. One MiG and one pilot "disintegrated." And yet, during the Cold War, the Cubans did not blame the United States for the attack. They must have known, as the strange scenario played out, that they were not dealing with the United States, that the destruction of the MiG and the death of its pilot were the act of alien forces. Thank goodness they had the good honest sense to realize that.

Radio broadcaster and ufologist Frank Edwards "apparently died of a heart attack" June 22, 1967 (Sprague 2014). He was the author of *Flying Saucers—Serious Business* and the host of the *Strangest of All* radio show (Sprague).

Considering the culture of Edwards' time, his heart attack was probably the result of obesity, smoking, and too much alcohol. This hypothesis could be totally incorrect, but it is testable. Was Edwards overweight? Did he smoke cigarettes? How much alcohol did he consume regularly? These questions can, hypothetically, be confirmed or denied.

So am I debunking Edwards' death as the result of nefarious forces? Not at all. I posit that Frank Edwards was driven to extremes of eating, smoking, and drinking not only because of the social behavior of the times but, ultimately, by the Gray aliens. They obviously did not care for Edwards' book or radio show.

Reports of UFOs investigating nuclear weapons or power plants are common occurrences. In extreme cases, intercontinental ballistic missiles (ICBMs) have been shut down. But the most terrifying cases of UFOs interacting with nuclear technology are the ones in which the UFO has activated ICBMs and prepared to launch.

In July of 1967, a UFO flew over Minot Air Force Base in North Dakota, and activated one of the nuclear missiles. The ICBM control flashed "Launch in Progress." Acting very quickly, missile controllers hit an inhibit switch, and the missile returned to its resting state. A similar event occurred in the Soviet Union in October 1982, involving the activation of multiple missiles (Maloney 2011).

Some who have experienced UFOs messing with nukes believe that the aliens are sending us a message—that nuclear weapons are too dangerous and we should destroy them before we destroy ourselves with them. But I totally disagree. Switching on a nuclear missile to "Launch in Progress" is an attack on a potentially massive scale. The Grays are not warning us, they are letting us know, in no uncertain terms, that they are impervious to our greatest destructive technologies and that they can destroy us with our own weapons. That's a threat, not a warning.

Rounding out the year of weird, Snippy the horse became the first reported case of animal mutilation. The horse was found dead and mutilated on September 7, 1967 (www.snippy.com). Though it was not a mutilation exactly typical of what has become the animal mutilation phenomenon, Snippy was connected to UFOs from the start. Nellie Lewis, Snippy's owner, was always convinced of the UFO connection.

"Snippy," such a chipper name for the advent of such horrors to come, not only led to cattle "mutes," strange lights preceding animal mutilations, and unmarked helicopters flying over mute sites, but the graduation to human mutilations. Torturing and killing animals is often the precursor to torturing and killing human beings. That psychological fact applies as much to the Grays as to anyone afflicted with inhumaneness and psychopathy.

1968

In August 1968, a CIA-led military team infiltrated North Vietnam on a mission to assassinate communist leaders. The team heard the guns of the North Vietnamese soldiers engaged in a desperate firefight with a UFO. The UFO fired a beam at the North Vietnamese, then departed over the ocean. The North Vietnamese soldiers were gone, and their weapons were in their place, melted (Maloney 2011).

Again, how and why did a UFO pick a side in a conflict? The communists did fire on the UFO. Perhaps this was one of those cases when the UFO decided to fire back instead of speed off.

1975

Whenever the history of alien abductions is presented, you can bet on hearing two names, Hill and Walton. Everyone in ufology is familiar with these cases. My "second next book" should be subtitled *And No Travis Walton*, simply because the case is so overexposed and polarized. There really are basically two camps in the Travis Walton case: those who believe him and those who think he is a liar and a hoaxer. I fall into the first camp. And I do not have much to add to this case, except to point out that a fairly remarkable and unique instance took place on the evening of November 5, 1975, near Turkey Springs, Arizona. Yes, Travis Walton was abducted for five days, and yes, his companions largely passed polygraphs. But I am not interested in those aspects of the case.

Travis Walton was attacked. Naïve curiosity led Walton to get out of the truck and approach the UFO. Even as it began to wobble more and emit a building whine, Travis stood before it in awe and expectation. But he did not expect it to attack him. The craft fired a beam of light that hit Travis Walton in the face and chest and blew him back several feet. When his companions left him on the ground, the driver was reacting with an appropriate fear response of flight. The men had seen Travis get shot and then his motionless body on the ground. They assumed, wisely, that he was dead and there was nothing to do for him. Travis Walton got shot by a UFO and his companions didn't want to be next.

1976

March 1976, White Sands Missile Test Range: Air Force Sergeant Jonathan Louette is abducted from the base and his body found in the desert three days later. Louette had been mutilated in the exact same fashion as cattle. He had been exsanguinated, his anus had been cored out, and the lower intestine removed, the eyes were missing, tongue had been cut from his throat, glands in the neck were missing, and his sexual organs were gone—all with a surgical precision that suggested highly advanced medical equipment and procedure, such as lasers with suction devices for cutting "cookie-cutter" holes into the victim, usually for the removal of glands.

Two other gruesome cases occurred in Brazil and Egypt. A man was mutilated in Brazil, his prostate removed through the penis. A family of six in Egypt were mutilated in the same fashion as the rest of the newly emerging human mutilation cases, a worldwide phenomenon.

1977

In 1977, UFOs attacked the villagers of Colares, Brazil, with beam weapons, similar to the 1886 attack in Venezuela. The villagers called the attacking UFOs "chupa-chupas," roughly, "bloodsuckers" because when the beams hit them, they could feel themselves being drained of their blood. The villagers were injured by the bright beams and "suffered burns, blood loss, paralysis or small wounds." Dr. Wellaide, head of Colares Hospital, observed "crise nervosa" in her chupa-chupa attack patients (basically nervous breakdowns), as well as "partial paralysis of the body," "headaches, debility, dizziness, generalized tremors...first-degree burns marked by tiny perforations." Many other surrounding villages experienced identical attacks (Dembeck 2012).

The Brazilian attacks of late 1977 are troubling in many ways. First, the beam attacks were painful and caused various maladies resembling radiation sickness. And also first, the Grays targeted and attacked poor people, those least able to defend themselves.

1978

October 21, 1978: pilot Frederick Valentich's Cessna 182 departs Melbourne at 6:19 p.m. Below 5000 feet Valentich reports seeing "a large aircraft" (Redfern 2014). His reports during the incident tell the tale:

> It seems to me that he's playing some sort of game...flying over me two to three times at speeds I could not identify...it's flying past, it's a long shape...it seems like it's chasing me...the thing is just orbiting on top of me...It's got a green light and sort of metallic. It's all shiny...Approaching from the southwest...engine is rough idling...that strange aircraft is hovering on top of me... hovering and it's not an aircraft (Redfern).

And with a punctuated burst of static, Valentich and his Cessna were lost forever. The pilot's transcript is absolutely clear that a genuine UFO was responsible for his disappearance. He might have been blasted from the sky by some kind of electromagnetic pulse weapon, which would account for the burst of static heard in the control tower. Further, an electromagnetic weapon could also account for Valentich's announcement that his engine was "rough idling" and would have resulted in his plane shutting off completely. Valentich then would have found himself plummeting to the earth. But no remains were ever found.

Perhaps Valentich's dead Cessna was taken inside the UFO with Valentich as abductee—one of those who are taken and never returned. Or perhaps Valentich met a fate similar to Captain Mantell, only this time the beam vaporized the pilot and plane. Either way, Valentich's fate was not a pleasant one.

1979

As predicted by the FBI, the animal mutilation cases did enter a new phase in 1979: the first reported human mutilation case. (In fact, other earlier human mutilation events occurred, but were not as high profile as this case.) Two hunters in Idaho found a man who had been mutilated in the same manner and with the surgical precision seen in the cattle mutes (Redfern 2014).

1980

Huffman, Texas, 9:00 p.m., December 29, 1980: Vickie Landrum, her grandson, and Betty Cash encountered a UFO that emitted enormous levels of mutagenic radiation, light, and intense heat. The close encounter lasted just under an hour, but it was time and proximity enough to irradiate the three victims. "They suffered from dehydration, severe diarrhea, headaches, incessant sickness, and an inability to keep anything liquid or solid down" (Redfern 2014). Further, Betty Cash was the most severely irradiated and suffered also from "sores… all across her body" and "her hair began to fall out" (Redfern). She developed breast cancer and had both breasts removed. Betty Cash never recovered from her close encounter with the UFO. Not all death is sudden. Some murder takes "exactly 18 years" (Redfern).

Why would a UFO block a country road in Texas to irradiate three unremarkable humans? Did Vickie Landrum know more about the alien agenda than she has admitted? Was she helping the aliens with radiation experiments on her grandson? Did Betty Cash discover this? Was the close encounter a planned meeting to kill Betty Cash? No, of course not! This is all absolutely mad conjecture! And what about the Army helicopters that followed after the UFO in seeming pursuit—was this an experiment gone wrong and uncontained, or was it an alien craft pursued by military aircraft? But if it was a pursuit, why use CH-47 Chinook helicopters instead of faster and better armed jet aircraft?

1993

Ufologist Ron Rummel of Portland, Oregon, shot himself through the mouth on August 6, 1993 (Sprague 2014). Was he "suicided" or did he just kill himself because he lived in Portland? Portland, Oregon, was ranked the twelfth most "suicidal city" in the nation (businessinsider.com).

1996

January 17, 1996, the provocative Phil Schneider was suicided by hanging with catheter tubing around the neck; in fact, not just around the neck but "beneath the flaps of skin…wrapped around his neck three times before it was double knotted" (Sprague 2014). The action hero of the 1979 Dulce Base firefight, Schneider was famous for his inspired tale of entering into armed combat with Grays. He claimed to have shot and killed one with his Walther PPK. Schneider also claimed he had been shot by one of the aliens. In the famous YouTube video, Schneider holds up his hand to expose the missing fingers he says were vaporized. He claims the beam also hit him in the chest and "splayed him open."

Imagine an alien assassination squad appearing in Schneider's residence. They paralyze the large man and begin the gruesome task of threading catheter tubing beneath his skin around his neck. The Grays hang him like a worn garment. You cannot just kill a Gray and get away with it. They understand revenge.

2003

In August 2003, Todd Sees of Northumberland, Pennsylvania, set out in the morning on his quad to find good hunting spots for deer. He told his wife he would be home by noon, but his day was about to get really, really bad. Todd Sees parked his quad near a power pole; witnesses reported a UFO hovering over the pole, a light coming from its underside, and the shape of a man rising up in the light. When noon came and went, Todd Sees' wife called the police. A major search effort found Todd Sees in some brush the next day—an area already searched, which means he was killed and deposited in the brush after the first day of searching. His body was dressed only in underwear. One of his boots was discovered high in a tree. Todd Sees was callously murdered by Grays, and then dumped to rot.

The twenty-first century has seen a shift in UFO perceptions. Perhaps, at least in the United States, this shift to a darker interpretation of UFOs is due to the attacks of 9/11, the event that made cynics of optimists and killed lingering naivety of Pax Americana. Not to say that UFOs were not dangerous and malicious from day one of encounters—the aliens have always been little Gray bastards—but the horror of 9/11 allowed for the consideration of ufology's very, very dark side.

The Grays have been responsible for so much human suffering that it's difficult to say which attack is worse than another. Certainly, human mutilation (while the victim is conscious, no less) is at the top of the list. But what about global murder?

I have always accepted as axiom that if the Grays are technologically superior enough for interstellar and possibly interdimensional travel, then fixing a rapidly dying biosphere should be simple science for them. During abduction events, the Grays are known often to show abductees images of a ravaged planet, killed by resource rape and nuclear war. Most abductees interpret this vision as a warning and a call to action. But the Grays know that our environmental crisis is a mass-extinction event and that we humans have no way to return the living world to pre-Industrial environmental homeostasis. By not helping, the Grays are committing…what?! Is there even a word for this crime of negligence? Perhaps it has been coined before, but "Gaiacide" may suffice, the effective genocide of a planet's entire biosphere. Of course, the human race is ultimately responsible (beginning with the advent of agriculture), but we are a giant organism comprised of over seven billion human beings, rolling stupidly across the earth, killing everything. Seriously, what do we expect of ourselves?

Yes, the Grays attack. But is their violence against us different from the violence we inflict upon each other? The Grays have abducted, mutilated, and murdered millions of people, and done nothing to prevent the extinction of the human species.

So have people. How alien a species we are to each other.

CHAPTER ELEVEN

PARANOIA MELTDOWN TO CONCLUSION

O ne night in 1982, shortly before Earl and his family left California, he had a dream that he says felt "prophetic" to him. In the dream he was driving around Southern California in an older model station wagon, the back of which was filled with hundreds of copies of UFO booklets.

In this dream, I was the author of these self-published books about UFOs and I was taking them around to bookstores all over the Los Angeles area where I placed them for sale on consignment. This dream was very significant to me, as if it were conveying an important message that this is what I was meant to do: to write and sell books about UFOs. Of course, when I woke up and thought about it rationally, I realized it actually was a terrible idea. The authors of UFO books, especially books published at the author's own expense and sold out of the trunk of their car, are looked upon as crackpots. It was the last thing I should do if I wanted to live a sensible life. But the dream stayed with me, and later, after we got settled in Oregon, I came to believe that writing UFO books was something that maybe I was destined to do."

And do it, he did. In 1985, Earl wrote and self-published two short nonfiction works about UFOs. The first of these was a brief summary of Heriot's personal speculations about the possible nature, origins, and motives of so-called "alien" UFO occupants. He offered copies at discount to Hank Martin (pseudonym), a mail-order book dealer who put out a monthly catalog of new and used UFO-related books for sale. Martin bought multiple copies of this first booklet from Earl and sold them through his catalog, eventually selling out the small edition of 100 or fewer copies. Earl followed this modest success with a longer work that analyzed a classic UFO crash retrieval case in considerable detail. As with the first book, Hank Martin ordered copies of Earl's second book and it too sold slowly but steadily, the pair of books earning Earl some much needed extra income.

Earl explains that, in those days, there was still a strong stigma attached to UFO literature that went beyond basic reports of hardware sightings and into the more suspect literary territory of alleged alien contact and abduction. As a writer, he felt it was safer for him to stay away from anything that smacked of contact, a policy that factored into his decision not to publish his report, already written, of the Long Beach Blimp UFO. Speculative works free of any personal claims, and "at arm's distance" works of historical summary and analysis seemed less risky to Earl than anything that suggested he not only believed that aliens existed but that he had contact with them. In a word, he was "comfortable" putting out books that played with weird ideas in general, but that didn't go the distance in terms of making personal claims of unexplained or paranormal experience.

In 1985, Earl drafted a third UFO-related booklet, this one another work of speculation. Where it differed from his first book is that it was more about the nature of reality itself, and how that shapes our understanding and experience of the UFO phenomenon, and less about "What are those darned aliens up to, anyway?" It was wilder, crazier, more "out there" than the first book. Still, he didn't think it was particularly risky, or that it would provoke any kind of negative feedback or focus unwanted attention on him. As far as he was concerned, it was just another harmless little UFO booklet of which he hoped he could sell a handful of copies.

Earl sent a proof copy of this third booklet to Hank Martin to get the book dealer's opinion of it before having the edition printed. Miller's reaction shocked and profoundly disturbed Heriot. It was something he was totally unprepared for, and it shook him to his core. Holding Miller's long typewritten letter in his hands, Earl says he literally trembled in fear. Some idea expressed in Earl's new text had touched a raw nerve. Now he was getting feedback on that, but not from Hank. Hank was merely the channel, the medium for the feedback. The feedback was from THEM—the aliens themselves!—and they gave him an earful about this new book. There was something in it that they did not like at all, and that they did not agree with, and they were angry, as angry as a hive of buzzing hornets. Earl says he hasn't reread the letter since 1985, so he doesn't recall the details, but the effect it had on him was unforgettable.

I asked Earl if he still had that letter from Hank Miller, and if I could see it. He did, and he let me read it.

The letter, dated in early November 1985, is indeed very strange and more than a little creepy, but I think Earl overreacted to it. In the letter, Hank Martin told Earl in no uncertain terms that there were ideas in the book that he found unacceptable. But, oddly enough, they were not Earl's quirky and at times bizarre theories about the nature of reality and the origin and motives of aliens. What Martin objected to was Earl's use of specific words that Martin viewed as evidence of his having a negative frame of mind. In making this criticism, Martin sounded like a follower of some religious cult, a brow-beaten disciple who had been brainwashed by his masters into picking apart every word spoken by the outsiders and infidels who had not accepted the wisdom of the group's teachings. Martin explained that over a period of eighteen months, he routinely received long telephone calls from an unknown person who lectured him on various philosophical and metaphysical principles, including the importance of not succumbing to negative thoughts. According to Martin, over time his brain was rewired by these lectures and his behavior changed to such a degree that his wife took the kids and left him. Martin said that for much of this period he was unsure if he was listening to a human being, an alien, or a robot—the language used was so perfect and it was delivered without pause or hesitation. Only when the lecturer stopped once to cough did Martin decide he was listening to another person and not an alien. Martin never came out and said that the teachings he was being subjected to originated with the aliens, but he did say that he learned from the mysterious caller that human society is under the control of "other intelligences" and he implied that these intelligences would deal harshly with anyone who attempted to expose them for what they are. Martin implied that he would use the mental clarity he had gained through this process to write about (and expose?) the aliens, but he also said that the training freed him from traditional human patterns of thought, leaving him mentally "empty" and ready to move on to a new way of life. Did he mean by this that he was thinking more like an alien and less like a human being?

I can see why Earl was panicked by this letter. It's creepy and off-putting. After rereading it several times, I decided the letter probably doesn't suggest that the aliens took exception to something Earl had written. Earl was mistaken on that point. Rather, it suggests that Hank Martin was under the influence of persons or forces unknown—possibly malevolent forces that Earl was wise to avoid engaging.

Upon receipt of this letter, Earl canceled the publication of his third UFO book, broke off contact with Hank Martin, sold his collection of over 300 UFO books and even his sci-fi books (many of which dealt with aliens fictionally), and abandoned all research on UFOs and aliens. Earl calls this episode his "paranoia meltdown."

This was the second time Earl Heriot had gotten rid of a large collection of UFO books. The first time was when he sold his original UFO library to college buddy John Silver after constant nagging. Over the following several years

Earl had painstakingly rebuilt the collection, book by book, until he had replaced all of the titles except for a few rare ones that proved impossible to locate. And later, in the years following his "paranoia meltdown," he again rebuilt the collection, finding new copies of all but the rarest titles for his third UFO library. This last collection he intends to keep permanently.

"Yeah," he admits:

I probably overreacted. The letter really freaked me out. It made my skin crawl. Up to that point, I had played with the idea of believing in aliens, but I hadn't fully accepted it as fact that they actually were real. It was an open-ended question with me, and I wasn't looking too hard for an answer. But when Hank Martin told me about those eerie phone calls, the weird machine-like voice on the other end of the line lecturing him week after week, that made the idea of aliens suddenly very real. Something from outside our normal, everyday reality had reached out and contacted Martin, and I was terrified they would contact me, too. I wanted nothing to do with that. I swore to myself—and to them, assuming that they knew everything I thought and did—that if they would just leave me the hell alone, I would keep my mouth shut and not write anything else about them. It was like a deal you make with God, a silent oath. So, I ended my brief career as a UFO author and they seemed to more or less leave me alone after that.

Earl Heriot's third UFO book remains unpublished to this day. Over the years, he has given a few proof copies to friends but aside from that, it is an aborted publication, suppressed by its author out of fear of what unknown forces might do if he should ever make it public.

I asked Earl how he might react if he received a letter like that today, given a similar situation.

If that happened now, I think my reaction would be quite different. I would consider Hank Martin to be someone I could not trust enough to do business with, and I would distance myself from him, but I wouldn't necessarily change my publishing plans based entirely on a vague, rambling letter like that, regardless of how spooky it seemed. It's amazing to me that Martin allowed himself to be indoctrinated over an extended period of time by an unknown person with unknown motives—or if the lecturer's motives were in fact known to Martin, he didn't bother to tell me about it.

I have to think Martin may have been "played" by his teacher, convinced to change his way of thinking almost against his will, or at least without informed consent, and that the teacher may have been tasked by either a human organization representing aliens, or by the aliens themselves, with redirecting Martin's energies away from his UFO book distribution business, which to some degree was helping spread the truth about alien activities, and towards a freelance writing career, which likely would be less effective in getting the word out about the alien threat. At one point in the letter, Martin relates that the voice on the phone told him he was a "genius" at communicating, and said that he was wasting his time with the book-selling business. This combination of flattery and insult was clearly intended to get him to change what he was doing with his life—possibly for the benefit of the alien agenda. I have to wonder if Martin wasn't, in fact, under the control of what contactee George Adamski called "the silence group," a nefarious shadow organization that works to keep the public in the dark about the reality of the alien presence on Earth. In the letter, Martin urged me to join the program and change my own way of thinking. He warned I might lose my friends and family in the process. Back then, that freaked me out. Now, my answer would be "Thanks, but no thanks!" and "Adiós, pal!" I think I would see him as the pathetic tool of a cult, or worse, and I wouldn't let him dictate what I would or would not do.

Shortly after Earl wrote to Martin announcing his retirement from ufology, he got a letter back in which Martin said he was surprised that his last letter caused such a strong reaction in Earl and that he didn't intend it to be a warning against Earl's writing about aliens, but he didn't go as far as apologizing and said he would have written the same letter even had he known that Earl might take it the wrong way. Martin then tells a fascinating story about another acquaintance of his who reacted negatively in a similar way and abandoned his paranormal researches when he experienced a series of bizarre and disturbing synchronicities immediately after meeting the 1950s contactee Orfeo Angelucci, in the 1970s. Much like Earl did, the researcher disposed of his "world-class library" on the paranormal, dumping the books in the trash.

Martin goes on to speculate that Earl might someday return to ufology when he's had time to cool off, explaining that some of us are cursed or blessed with an innate interest in the unknown, and it's a difficult thing to suppress over the long haul. In this he was correct; Earl Heriot did eventually resume passively studying UFOs, but he managed to restrain himself from overtly writing about the subject, at least in nonfictional form.

Earl Heriot's life became peaceful again once he swore off publishing UFO books. He continued his hobby of writing fiction and poetry as he always had and, as in the past, some of these new works were horror stories in which the "monsters" were thinly disguised aliens or malign spiritual entities from other dimensions "outside" our mundane world. I've read these stories and believe that the alien plot elements they contain may represent suppressed UFO-related experiences residing in Earl's subconscious mind that are "leaking" into his consciousness through the medium of fiction. In other words, although the stories are made up, the hostile beings he writes of may be real ones that he has encountered at various times in his life. The stories, with their haunted moods and settings, are perhaps a way for him to deal with the uncertainty and fear these entities cause in him, a way for him to put his deep anxiety to rest. I asked him if this might be the case.

"Perhaps," he answered, "or maybe I just enjoy making up weird stories."

In the years following his "meltdown," Earl had a few unusual sightings and experiences, although there was nothing of the magnitude of his Long Beach Blimp UFO incident. One of these sightings happened when he was camping with his family in a tent at Detroit Lake in Oregon in the late 1980s. They were in a crowded campground, not isolated in the woods or anything scary like that, but when he got up in the middle of the night to use the public restroom, he was very "creeped out" while walking alone down the trail to the restrooms. There wasn't another person in sight as he rushed along in the dark with his flashlight playing over the ground. About halfway to the restroom, he happened to look up at the portion of sky visible between the trees overhead and was startled to see a massive white "cloud" floating high over him; the cloud-like object was symmetrically shaped in the image of a Native American Thunderbird symbol. It passed by quickly and made no sound. The symmetry of the cloud's shape was unnaturally perfect, with square-edged zig-zag lines outlining the two wings of the Thunderbird; the wings were perfect mirror images of one another.

> There was no way this was a natural cloud. It had a deliberate design to it. Either it was an artificial flying craft, or I was having a mystical vision. I was completely awed by this thing but it didn't frighten me. I didn't sense any hostility from it. It was just weird and unexpected. After I peed, I beat it back to the tent and was glad to be back inside, zipping up the flap. I didn't tell my wife about it. Why ruin her sleep with a spooky story?

I have to wonder if this might be an instance of unrecognized alien abduction. Is Earl remembering only the beginning and ending parts of the experience, with the middle part (the actual abduction) neatly edited out by the aliens, using whatever form of mind control or induced amnesia they employ to keep their victims from suspecting what has happened? If that's the case, it seems the walk from the tent to where he first saw the "Thunderbird" in the night sky would be the beginning of the experience, and then his hasty walk to the restroom and back to the tent would be the ending. Earl didn't look at his watch before or after the sighting and his family slept through the entire incident, so there's no way of knowing if there is any unexplained missing time. What is highly suggestive of an abduction scenario, however, is that he felt an inappropriate amount of fear while walking through a well-populated campground full of peacefully sleeping people. What did he think was going to happen? Did he somehow sense a genuine threat lurking out there in the darkness? I asked him if he was always that afraid when he got up at night to use the restroom while camping.

No, not like that. It's always a bit strange, of course, but I've never had that degree of terror from it. Only that one time. It's like I knew I was going to see something freaky, and then I did.

During the late 1980s and continuing into the 1990s, Earl Heriot had a number of strange dreams at night in which he felt a threatening presence in his bedroom. The feeling that someone was there was so strong it roused him out of a deep sleep and into a state of being partially awake and physically aware of the room around him but not awake enough to open his eyes and see if anything was there. In some of these "dreams" he was so terrified he literally hid his head under the covers until the fear passed or he fell asleep again. Common to these dreams is that in each instance he sensed that there were several "beings" in the house, not just a single intruder, and something about their "presence" made him suspect that aliens were approaching his bed. He says:

This happened maybe a dozen times over several years. I never opened my eyes and saw them in the room. I couldn't tell you how tall they were, the shape of their heads, the color of their eyes. Nothing like that. I would suddenly sense "They're here!" and a tidal wave of fear would wash over me. Then I would drift off into blackness, a dreamless sleep, and wake up perfectly calm a couple hours later, the "visitation" forgotten. By morning, it was like it never happened. I never wrote down anything about it, not even a short note, and I didn't bother to pay attention to it when it happened, or how often it happened. I couldn't even guess at a year or range of years, but the general sense I have is that it didn't start until several years after the paranoia meltdown, and it continued into the 1990s. I think by the 2000s, it was a thing of the past, and it hasn't happened since.

Earl says that during this period there were other, possibly related experiences where he would wake up at about 3:00 a.m. hearing what he called "some kind of demented Calliope music." This happened five or six times over a period of about two years.

It sounded like it was not inside our house but nearby, and it was moving around the neighborhood, coming closer, moving away. The music—if that's what it was—sounded completely insane, like something out of a horror movie set at a carnival. And it was loud. I couldn't believe it didn't wake up the whole neighborhood. I had this idea that it had to be that loud to hide the screams of the people who were being abducted where the music was playing. I pictured this huge carrousel-like UFO that was in the middle of the street, twirling like mad, with lights flashing and the crazy music streaming out of it full blast. The sound scared the hell out of me, and I don't know why. As with the visitors-in-the-room dreams, I would be really terrified and then I'd fall asleep and wake up later feeling quite calm and peaceful. Again, I never made any written documentation on these strange night sounds, and I can't assign them to any particular year. I'm just glad they eventually ended.

Earl's wife Jane always slept through these nocturnal terrors and has no knowledge of them. Earl didn't want to frighten her needlessly and has never told her about the odd experiences.

Early one evening about 5:00 p.m. during the 1990s, Earl Heriot was in front of his house in Salem, facing east, when he spotted a large ball of red light in the sky a short distance above the horizon. It rapidly descended vertically and disappeared below the skyline of trees and rooftops. He says it was too large to be the running lights from a conventional aircraft, although the Salem Municipal Airport is located about three miles east of his house, and the object was an estimated two or three miles away, placing it near or at the airport. The object glowed a dull red hue, "like a red-hot poker." The sighting lasted for only a few seconds. Earl says the object was the relative (angular) size of the moon. As with other incidents during this period, he made no written record of the sighting and can't assign it to any particular year.

A second unusual sighting, dating to sometime in the 1990s, occurred one night about 9:00 p.m. when Earl, Jane, and their youngest daughter were walking home after having visited Liza Henry (pseudonym), a neighbor friend who lived a half block away from the Heriots. As the Heriots reached the street corner opposite their house, Earl happened to look up and saw a tight formation of three triangular-shaped objects passing immediately overhead. They were completely unlit and Earl says the only reason he was able to see them was due to the faint reflection of ambient city light off the smooth underside of the objects. The objects were each the size of a small jet and were a grayish-silver color. He detected no markings on them, and they did not have a fuselage, each craft consisting of simply a triangular wing form with rounded corners. They were visible for only a second or two before disappearing into the clouds, the night being overcast. Earl became excited and tried to point out the objects to his wife and daughter, but neither of them looked up in time to see them. Earl believes they were flying at a low altitude of about 200 feet. The objects emitted no exhaust trail and were totally silent. Earl speculates these may have been secret military aircraft with an advanced swept wing design. Or, they may have been true unknowns—UFOs. Again, Earl made no written record of this sighting and didn't bother to note the date.

Earl Heriot's last remembered UFO-related event was a sighting that occurred sometime in the late 1990s or early 2000s. About 7:15 a.m. one weekday morning, Earl was standing at a bus stop across from his house. High above him in the sky, slightly to the west, he saw a so-called "chemtrail" running from north to south, horizon to horizon. This, in itself, was not unusual; Earl had started noticing oddly persistent jet contrails in the 1980s, and had become used to seeing them in the skies over Oregon several days a week. What caught his attention on that particular morning, however, was something highly unusual. What he took to be a large aircraft was hanging in midair very close to the chemtrail, on the side nearest to Earl.

At first, Earl thought the object must be flying straight at him, so that there was no apparent motion, and he expected it to increase in relative size as it continued to approach. Several minutes went by and the relative size of the object did not change. That suggested it wasn't moving after all, that it was hovering in a stationary position alongside the chemtrail. By that time, he had become aware of the object's unconventional triangular shape and realized it was large enough to be a military bomber. Its shape and size made it superficially resemble the Northrup Flying Wing experimental aircraft built during the 1940s. Like the three smaller triangular objects he had seen before, this object had no distinct fuselage. The object was dark gray and he didn't notice any running lights on it.

Earl was intent on continuing to watch the strange object until it did something—either fly away or disappear— but at 7:25 or so, his bus pulled up and he forced himself to get on, not wanting to be late for work. From his seat inside the bus, he didn't have a view of the aerial object and thus he has no idea of how the situation ultimately ended. Earl speculates that:

> What I saw may have been a man-made aircraft, some secret test design, and perhaps it was studying or monitoring the chemtrail, taking measurements or whatever. On the other hand, it might have been an alien craft, curious about the chemical makeup of the trail. Maybe it was taking samples. It was a weird sight, a chemtrail with a UFO next to it, just hanging there. I've seen plenty of chemtrails, but this is the only time there was a UFO present and checking out the chemtrail.

He never saw another UFO and had no bizarre experiences where he felt what he calls "the presence of aliens" since the possible nocturnal visitations of the 1980s and '90s. He says, "It's like they lost interest in me or something, and now they're leaving me alone. That's fine with me. I hope it stays this way."

At the beginning of my discussion of Earl Heriot's lifelong history of unexplained experiences, mysterious memories, and strange mental images, I explained that he sees himself as an open-minded observer of the UFO phenomenon. After looking at his testimony in detail, it seems to me that in summary there are a few things I can state about Earl Heriot's story. Whatever the nature of these experiences, this is something that has been happening to Earl for most of his life, from early childhood until about ten years ago, with events that he recalls falling into the 1950s, 1960s, 1970s, 1980s, 1990s, and early 2000s. It's not a short-term, temporary thing. Earl has witnessed, or endured, a half-century of alien phenomena.

The personal history Earl has shared with us only represents what he consciously remembers. Other incidents similar to these may lay buried in his subconscious mind, especially if we accept the possibility that aliens are able to exert a form of mind control over humans that suppresses their ability to remember selected parts of their sightings of UFOs and encounters with aliens. This could be done by the aliens through the use of technology, or through some form of mental control they themselves have over humans. I believe that if Earl agreed to undergo hypnotic regression, he would recover memories of additional experiences beyond those of which he is currently aware, as well as gain a more detailed narrative about and insight into the experiences he does recall without hypnosis. As I wrote earlier, he's not willing to be regressed and would rather not know all of the details of his UFO experiences.

"Maybe I just got too old to be of interest to them anymore," he speculates. "Younger subjects may deliver more pay-off, especially if their primary interest in us is genetics, hybrid breeding, emotional vampirism, etcetera."

There's another possibility, one that Earl had already considered—perhaps the experiences continue as before, but he simply isn't remembering them now. In this scenario, the forced amnesia has become perfect, and all memories of the events are being blocked from Earl's conscious mind. If that's the case, it would likely come out during hypnosis, which is another reason why he may be better off not being regressed, and not knowing the truth.

Heriot thinks it just might kill him:

> So I go and get hypnotically regressed and something horrible comes out, and I start getting really scared and paranoid. Say, I probably get rid of all my UFO books again. I'm already terrified and paranoid, thanks to you. What you wrote about my experiences really freaked me out—I haven't been this afraid of aliens in years! David, you and I are friends, and I'm telling you as a friend that we need to stop this now. I'm serious. No more. All of these interviews have really put our friendship through the wringer. Now I associate you with the aliens, because you're the one always asking the questions! It'll be even worse for me when your book comes out. Go ahead and publish it, though. I'm just really worried that I'll get abducted and end up a mute. [Editor: a victim of mutilation by aliens.] Your story of "Earl Heriot" could end like that, and you know it. So let's just end it with this telephone call, okay?

LITTLE GRAY BASTARDS

Grays commonly show apocalyptic images to abductees. This has been interpreted variously as an environmental and anti-nuclear warning to humankind. But the doomsday movies are nothing so compassionate as a warning. The Grays are sadists and enjoy the human emotions that come from seeing our planet destroyed. Recently, I have experienced three powerful images of my home and neighborhood as they appear after nuclear war and environmental collapse.

The first vision, I was parking my car in front of my house, and it was a brilliant summer day, very hot. Suddenly my vision "flickered" and I saw the suburban street transformed. The light was a bright yet sickly yellow. All the vegetation was gone—no trees, bushes, lawns—just the baked dry clay earth, cracked and lifeless. Sedimentation had begun, with the dust encrusting everything. Dirt devils spun ferociously. Many cars remained, forever parked in front of the neglected crumbling houses, caked with dust and rusting down to the broken pavement.

Forever the face of the Gray. *Digital illustration and photography by Mark Madland, 2014*

The second vision, I was in the living room, looking out the large window onto the street. A tornado was busting straight down the block, tearing down trees and sucking up flowerbeds. My mom was looking out the window when a smaller twister broke off and tore up all the vegetation in front of the house. I heard her scream, just as if she and I were really there in that storm, "Oh, no! My berm!"

The third vision, I was sitting in the sun in the backyard with my mom when suddenly the lawn disappeared. All of the vegetation was gone. The soil had completely desiccated and was broken by deep cracks into a backyard landscape of sunbaked clay. The air was thick with dust. Nothing seemed to be living.

Perhaps Dr. Oliver Sacks would categorize these visions as hallucinations, and he would be correct. I did hallucinate all three visions. The questions of relevance are, "Why did I have these very specific hallucinations? Are they an ecstatic truth to tell from the not-too-distant future? Where did the visions originate?"

I do not believe that I am psychic. I am, however, extremely sensitive. This sensitivity has developed into limited precognitive abilities. I believe my visions of a post-apocalyptic neighborhood came from the Grays and that my own imagination was the conduit to the future that brought on the visions. When I am most reflective on this I can recall my childhood in which I grew up terrified of nuclear annihilation, lying in bed sleepless and panicking for hours in the dark. Were the Grays there with me then, as well, feeding me images of mushroom clouds and ringing in the death knell of public emergency sirens? Probably. In any case, those visions were actual snapshots of a rapidly approaching human extinction event. Soon the droughts will devastate crops and we will starve by the millions, as increasingly desperate nations turn to nuclear war as policy, and the one percent hole up in their fortressed bunkers.

NO HELP IS COMING FROM THE LITTLE GRAY "BUCKING FASTARDS."

GLOSSARY

Abductee: Someone who believes he or she has been abducted (taken against their will) by alien beings. Abductions happen in secrecy and often involve pain and fear for the person who is taken. Examinations and medical procedures may be performed on the person without his or her permission. Afterwards, the person is made to forget the entire experience. Those who call themselves abductees usually consider it a negative, unwanted experience. They believe that aliens are evil, or at least indifferent about the welfare of the abducted person.

Apex Predator: The organism at the top of the food chain.

Biosphere: The sum total of all life forms and their interactions with each other and the non-living environment on a planetary scale.

Close Encounters of the Fourth Kind (CE-4): Alien abduction.

Close Encounters of the Fifth Kind (CE-5): Response from UFO to human desire for contact.

Close Encounters of the Sixth Kind (CE-6): Injury or death caused by a UFO.

Close Encounters of the Eighth Kind (CE-8): Aliens mentally control a human.

Close Encounters of the Tenth Kind (CE-10): Fighting back.

Contactee: Someone who claimed contact with alien beings during the 1950s, usually reported as a positive experience. Unlike modern abductees (beginning with the Betty and Barney Hill case in 1961), contactees generally believed they had participated willingly in the contact event, that the aliens were morally good, and that the purpose of the contact was to help humans advance spiritually. Contactees often described the aliens they met as being highly attractive humanoids with whom they engaged in pleasant and enlightening conversations. Unlike abductees, contactees felt they had full conscious recall of the events.

The Drake Equation: The Drake Equation is a simplified tool to make a subjective prediction concerning the number of technologically intelligent life forms extant in the galaxy today:

$$N = R \times fp \times ne \times fl \times fi \times fc \times L$$

- "**N**" is the number of technologically communicating species in the Milky Way Galaxy.
- "**R**" is the rate of suitable star formation per year.
- Variable "**fp**" is the percentage of suitable stars for planets.
- Variable "**ne**" is the number of Earth-like planets in suitable solar systems.
- Variable "**fl**" is the percentage of planets capable of life that develop life.
- Variable "**fi**" is the percentage of suitable planets where intelligence develops.
- Variable "**fc**" is the percentage of planets where intelligence develops technology capable of radio communication.
- "**L**" is the number of years a technological civilization survives until self-destruction and extinction.

Ecstatic Truth: Defined by film director Werner Herzog as the truth that emerges from art and dreams, not merely from isolated facts; antonym: the truth of the accountants.

Experiencer: Someone who believes he or she has been taken by aliens, but sees it in an overall positive light. They feel that aliens are not evil and are, in fact, spiritually advanced beings who take people for purposes that are good and will eventually benefit humans or aliens. "Experiencer" sometimes is used as a neutral term to avoid labeling the contact as either negative or positive (i.e., abductee or contactee).

Exsanguination: The complete removal of all blood from an animal.

Grays (or Greys): The most commonly reported type of alien in abduction accounts. Grays are so named for their gray-colored skin. They are usually described as shorter than most humans (although there is also a type known as Tall Grays), with long, spindly arms, and legs that are short in proportion to the arms. Their bodies show no muscular development and Grays appear physically weak. Grays have very large heads relative to their body size. The heads are shaped like an inverted teardrop, with a pointed chin. The eyes are large, oval or almond-shaped, and often described as wrapping around the head. The eyes are usually black and lack a pupil. The mouth, nose, and ears are minimal or altogether absent aside from rudimentary orifices. Grays have no body hair, and no visible genitals. Grays were first reported in the early 1960s.

The Greada Treaty: As drafted by President Eisenhower and the Grays in 1954, the Greada Treaty provided the United States with alien technology in exchange for alien autonomy to abduct and experiment upon United States citizens with impunity.

Humanoid: Any life form whose holotype exhibits typical human morphology, including a large head, a trunk, and a pair of arms and legs.

Hybrids (human-alien): Alleged hybrid creatures that bear a blending of alien and human biological characteristics. Hybrids are allegedly artificially bred by aliens using genetic material extracted from human abductees. Some abductees claim the hybrid fetus is carried to term in a human female. When it is fully developed, the hybrid infant is taken from the pregnant human mother by aliens during an abduction. Some abductees claim they have seen and held their hybrid children during subsequent abductions. The aliens' purpose in breeding hybrids is unknown but theories include the possibility that the hybrids will be used at a later date as overlords who will control humans after an alien conquest of the Earth. Some abductees report having sexual encounters with male or female hybrids, sometimes against their will.

Ley Line: A geographic line of active natural forces and high paranormal activity.

Mantid (or Insectoid) Alien: A type of alien being that resembles a large insect. The most commonly reported form of insectoid being is the Mantid, or "Praying Mantis" type. These are described as taller than humans, with insectoid bodies having thin limbs with insect-like joints and large heads with pointed chins. The eyes are large and dark, much like those of the Grays. Mantids are often reported as being involved in or overseeing medical procedures during abductions, in conjunction with Grays. Mantid aliens are thought to play an important role in the human-alien hybridization program.

Missing Time: The theory that a period of time that can't otherwise be accounted for during an apparently "routine" UFO sighting may represent an unsuspected and unremembered alien abduction. The "missing time" may be a few minutes, a few hours, or—in extreme cases—several days. The person who experiences missing time does not remember anything that transpired during the period in question, and often only realizes he or she may have been abducted by aliens after he or she is regressed by a therapist and made to relive the experience while under hypnosis. Having an episode of unexplained missing time is one of the signs that you may have been abducted and don't even know it. This widely reported phenomenon was brought to the attention of the public by Budd Hopkin's landmark 1981 book, *Missing Time*. It is presumed that the aliens have somehow "erased" the memory of the abduction from the abductee's conscious mind.

Neonate: Mature life form with morphological characteristics of a newborn human (e.g., large head to body size ratio); some Grays have been termed "Neonates."

Pair Bond: The psychosexual attraction that results in reproduction and parental care in some vertebrate species.

Paraphysical: Property of being in more than one state of being; sharing qualities of both the real and unreal worlds.

Screen Memory (or Screen Image): A false memory believed to be implanted by aliens to block the real memory of an abduction event from the person's consciousness. Abductees report seeing such images as owls, cows, wolves, deer, rabbits, cats, and other animals during instances of suspected alien abduction. A screen memory of non-threatening "owls" may be the last thing the person remembers before the start of a "missing time" event. The false screen memory replaces a real memory of having seen aliens. Another theory is that the mind of the abductee creates a screen memory to protect the person from the fear that would be caused by a real memory of encountering aliens.

SETI: The Search for Extraterrestrial Intelligence using, primarily, radio telescopes to scan for messages from space.

Theory of Mind: The attribution of intentionality to another person's mental state; e.g., "I thought that I knew what he was thinking" (three levels of intentionality).

VALIS: *VALIS* is the title of a 1981 science fiction novel by Philip K. Dick. The term "VALIS" refers to an artificial satellite placed into orbit around the Earth by aliens from the star Sirius. In the novel, the VALIS object transmits holographic images and telepathic information to humans on Earth using pink laser beams. The name "VALIS" is an acronym for "Vast Active Living Intelligence System." Dick claimed the premise of the novel was based on his own real-life experiences.

BIBLIOGRAPHY

The Book of Space Ships and their Relationship with Earth, by the God of a Planet Near Earth and Others. Clarkesburg, WV: Saucerian Publications, [nd].

FBI *"George Adamski File" BUFILE No. 100-395273.* [no location, no publisher, nd].

Adamski, George. *Flying Saucers Farewell.* New York, NY: Abelard-Schuman, 1961.

Adamski, George. *Inside the Space Ships.* New York, NY: Abelard-Schuman, 1955.

Alexander, John B. *UFOs: Myths, Conspiracies, and Realities.* New York, NY: Thomas Dunne Books, 2011.

Allen, W. Gordon. *Space-Craft From Beyond Three Dimensions: A New Vista of the Entirety from Which Emerges the UFO.* New York, NY: Exposition Press, 1959.

Allingham, Cedric. *Flying Saucer From Mars.* New York, NY: British Book Centre, 1955.

Angelucci, Orfeo. *Concrete Evidence.* Scotia, NY: Arcturus Book Service, 1983.

Angelucci, Orfeo. *Million Year Prophecy.* Scotia, NY: Arcturus Book Service, 1983.

Angelucci, Orfeo. *The Secret of the Saucers.* Amherst, WI: Amherst Press, 1955.

Arnold, Kenneth and Ray Palmer. *The Coming of the Saucers: A Documentary Report on Sky Objects that Have Mystified the World.* Amherst, WI: Privately Published by the Authors, 1952.

Barker, David. *Alien Autopsy Barbecue.* Salem, OR: Golden Posterity Press, 2013.

Barker, David. *Cigar Shaped Craft.* Salem, OR: End of Time Productions, 1985.

Barker, David. *Scenarios of Alien Visitation.* Salem, OR: Saucers Unlimited, 1985.

Barker, David and Jordan Hofer. *Chupacabra Chalupa—Bizarro Science Fiction Stories.* Salem, OR: Golden Posterity Press, 2013.

Barker, Gray. *Gray Barker's Book of Adamski.* Pt. Pleasant, WV: New Saucerian Books, 2014.

Barker, Gray. *They Knew Too Much about Flying Saucers.* New York, NY: Tower, 1967.

Barry, Bill. *Ultimate Encounter.* New York, NY: Pocket Books, 1978.

Beckley, Timothy Green. *UFOs Among the Stars.* New Brunswick, NJ: Global Communications, 1992.

Bender, Albert K. and Gray Barker. *Flying Saucers and the Three Men.* London: Neville Spearman, 1963.

Bennett, Colin. *Looking for Orthon; The Story of George Adamski, the First Flying Saucer Contactee, and How He Changed the World.* New York, NY: Paraview Press, 2001.

Bergier, Jacque and the Editors of INFO. *Extraterrestrial Intervention: The Evidence.* Chicago, IL: Henery Regnery Company, 1974.

Chicago, IL: Henery Regnery Company, 1974.

Berlitz, Charles and William L. Moore. *The Roswell Incident.* New York, NY: Grosset & Dunlap, 1980.

Bethurum, Truman. *Aboard a Flying Saucer.* Los Angeles, CA: DeVorss, 1954.

Bethurum, Truman and Timothy Green Beckley. *Messages from the People of the Planet Clarion: The True Experiences of Truman Bethurum.* New Brunswick, NJ: 1995.

Bethurum, Truman. *Truman Bethurum's Personal Scrapbook.* Scotia, NY: Robert C. Girard, 1982.

Binder, Otto O. *Flying Saucers Are Watching Us.* New York, NY: Belmont Books, 1968.

Birnes, William J. *Aliens in America: A UFO Hunter's Guide to Extraterrestrial Hotspots Across the U.S.* Avon, MA: Adams Media, 2010.

Blum, Ralph and Judy. *Beyond Earth: Man's Contact with UFOs.* New York, NY: Bantam Books, 1974.

Blumrich, Josef F. *The Spaceships of Ezekiel.* New York, NY: Bantam Books, 1974.

Brown, Courtney. *Cosmic Explorers: Scientific Remote Viewing, Extraterrestrials, and a Message for Mankind.* New York, NY: Signet, 2000.

Brown, Courtney. *Cosmic Voyage: A Scientific Discovery of Extraterrestrials Visiting Earth.* New York, NY: Penguin Books USA, 1996.

Bryan, C. D. B. *Close Encounters of the Fourth Kind.* New York, NY: Penguin Books USA, 1995.

Clark, Jerome and Loren Coleman. *The Unidentified: Notes Towards Solving the UFO Mystery.* New York, NY: Warner Paperback Library, 1975.

Conroy, Ed. *Report on Communion.* New York, NY: Avon Books, 1989.

Contreras, Jessie A. *The Short and Simple Practical Guide on How to Summon UFO's* [sic]. Los Angeles, CA: Jessie A. Contreras (Kindle edition), 2013.

Cooper, Milton William. *Behold a Pale Horse.* Flagstaff, AZ: Light Technology Publishing, 1991.

Corso, Col. Philip J. (Ret.) *The Day after Roswell.* New York, NY: Pocket Books, 1997.

Darwin, Charles. *On the Origin of Species.* Cambridge, MA: Harvard University Press, 2003 (1859).

David, Jay. *The Flying Saucer Reader.* New York, NY: The New American Library, 1967.

Dawkins, Richard. *The Magic of Reality.* New York, NY: Free Press, 2011.

Dembeck, Chet. *We Are Not Alone And They Are Not Our Friends*. Baltimore, MD: Chet Dembeck and Publisher of One, 2012.

Dimond, Brother Michael. *UFOs: Demonic Activity & Elaborate Hoaxes Meant to Deceive Mankind*. Fillmore, NY: Most Holy Family Monastery, 2009.

Dolan, Richard M. and Bryce Zabele. *A.D. After Disclosure*. Rochester, NY: Keyhole Publishing, 2010.

Downing, Barry. *The Bible and Flying Saucers*. New York, NY: Marlowe, 1997.

Druffel, Ann and D. Scott Rogo. *The Tujunga Canyon Contacts*. Englewood Cliffs, NJ: Prentice-Hall, 1980.

Edwards, Frank. *Flying Saucers—Serious Business*. New York, NY: Bantam Books, 1966.

Edwards, Frank. *Flying Saucers—Here and Now!* New York, NY: Lyle Stuart, 1967.

Eichar, Donnie. *Dead Mountain: The Untold True Story of the Dyatlov Pass Incident*. San Francisco, CA: Chronicle Books, 2013.

Elders, Lee J., Brit Nilsson-Elders, and Thomas K. Welch. *UFO: Contact from the Pleiades, Volume I*. Phoenix, AZ: Genesis III Productions, 1979.

Elders, Lee and Brit. *UFO...Contact from the Pleiades, Volume II*. Phoenix, AZ: Genesis III Productions, 1983.

Fawcett, Lawrence and Barry J. Greenwood. *Clear Intent: The Government Coverup of the UFO Experience*. Englewood Cliffs, NJ: Prentice-Hall, 1984.

Ferguson, William. *My Trip to Mars*. Potomac, MD: Cosmic Study Center, [no date].

Fowler, Raymond. *The Andreasson Affair*. New York, NY: Bantam Books, 1980.

Fowler, Raymond. *The Andreasson Affair, Phase Two*. Englewood Cliffs, NJ: Prentice-Hall, 1982.

Fowler, Raymond. *The Watchers: The Secret Design Behind UFO Abduction*. New York, NY: Bantam Books, 1990.

Fowler, Raymond. *The Watchers II*. Newberg, OR: Wild Flower Press, 1995.

Fowler, Raymond. *The Andreasson Legacy*. New York, NY: Marlowe, 1997.

Friedman, Stanton T. and Don Berliner. *Crash at Corona: The U.S. Military Retrieval and Cover-Up of a UFO*. New York, NY: Marlowe, 1994.

Friedman, Stanton T. and Kathleen Marden. *Captured! The Betty and Barney Hill UFO Experience*. Franklin Lakes, NJ: The Career Press, 2007.

Fry, Daniel W. *"The White Sands Incident" and "To Men of Earth"* New Combined Edition. [no location, no publisher, no date].

Fuller, John G. *Aliens in the Skies: The Scientific Rebuttal to the Condon Committee Report*. New York, NY: G. P. Putnam's Sons, 1969.

Fuller, John G. *The Interrupted Journey: Two Lost Hours "Aboard a Flying Saucer."* New York, NY: The Dial Press, 1966.

Fuller, John G. *Incident at Exeter: The Story of Unidentified Flying Objects over America Today*. New York, NY: G.P. Putnam's Sons, 1966.

Gaddis, Vincent H. *Mysterious Fires and Lights*. New York, NY: David McKay, 1967.

Gibbons, Gavin. *On Board the Flying Saucers* [original title: *They Rode in Space Ships*]. New York, NY: Paperback Library, 1957.

Good, Timothy. *Alien Update*. New York, NY: Avon Books, 1993.

Green, Gabriel and Warren Smith. *Let's Face the Facts about Flying Saucers*. New York, NY: Popular Library, 1967.

Hampsch, Reverend John H. *Devils and Demons: Fact or Fiction?* Goleta, CA: Queenship, 2002.

Hampsch, Reverend John H. *Poltergeists and Seven Types of Ghosts*. Goleta, CA: Queenship, 2008.

Heard, Gerald. *Is Another World Watching? The Riddle of the Flying Saucers*. New York, NY: Harper & Brothers, 1951.

Herzog, Werner. *Of Walking in Ice*. New York, NY: Free Association, 2007.

Hesemann, Michael and Philip Mantlep. *Beyond Roswell: The Alien Autopsy Film, Area 51, & the U.S. Government Coverup of UFOs*. New York, NY: Marlowe, 1997.

Hewes, Hayden and Brad Steiger. *UFO Missionaries Extraordinary*. New York, NY: Pocket Books, 1976.

Hill, Paul R. *Unconventional Flying Objects: A Scientific Analysis*. Charlottesville, VA: Hampton Roads, 1995.

Hobana, Ion and Julien Weverbergh. *UFO's from Behind the Iron Curtain*. New York, NY: Bantam Books, 1974.

Hofer, Jordan. "An Evolutionary Ufology Hypothesis." *MUFON UFO Journal*, no. 507 (2010): 12.

Hofer, Jordan. *Evolutionary Ufology*. Atglen, PA: Schiffer, 2013.

Hofer, Jordan. "From UFO disbeliever to believer." *Statesman Journal*, June 23, 2012, Section C, Final Edition.

Hopkins, Budd. *Art, Life and UFOs*. San Antonio, TX: Anomalist Books, 2009.

Hopkins, Budd. *Intruders: The Incredible Visitations at Copley Woods*. New York, NY: Ballantine Books, 1987.

Hopkins, Budd. *Missing Time: A Documented Study of UFO Abductions*. New York, NY: Berkley, 1981.

Hopkins, Budd. *Witnessed: The True Story of the Brooklyn Bridge UFO Abductions*. New York, NY: Pocket Books, 1996.

Howe, Linda Moulton. *An Alien Harvest: Further Evidence Linking Animal Mutilations and Human Abductions to Alien Life Forms*. Huntingdon Valley, PA: Linda Moulton Howe Productions, 1989.

Huyghe, Patrick. *The Field Guide to Extraterrestrials*. New York, NY: Avon Books, 1996.

Hymers, Dr. R. L., Jr. and David Shigekawa. *UFO's and Bible Prophecy.* Van Nuys, CA: Bible Voice, 1976.

Hynek, J. Allen and Jacques Vallee. *The Edge of Reality: A Progress Report on Unidentified Flying Objects.* Chicago, IL: Henry Regnery, 1975.

Hynek, Dr. J. Allen. *The Hynek UFO Report.* New York, NY: Dell, 1977.

Hynek, J. Allen, Imbrogno, Philip J., and Bob Pratt. *Night Siege: The Hudson Valley UFO Sightings.* St. Paul, MN: Llewellyn, 1998.

Hynek, J. Allen. *The UFO Experience: A Scientific Inquiry.* Chicago, IL: Henry Regnery, 1972.

Jacobs, David M. *Secret Life: Firsthand Accounts of UFO Abductions.* New York, NY: Simon & Schuster, 1992.

Jacobs, David M. *The Threat: The Secret Agenda: What the Aliens Really Want and How They Plan to Get It.* New York, NY: Simon & Schuster, 1998.

Jacobs, David Michael. *The UFO Controversy in America.* New York, NY: Signet, 1975.

Jeffries, Benjamin. *Lost in the Darkness: Life Inside the World's Most Haunted Prisons, Hospitals, and Asylums.* Atglen, PA: Schiffer, 2013.

Jessup, M. K. *The Case for the UFO.* New York, NY: Citadel Press, 1955.

Jessup, M. K. *The Expanding Case for the UFO.* New York, NY: Citadel Press, 1957.

Jordan, Debbie and Mitchell, Kathy. *Abducted!* New York, NY: Dell, 1994.

Jung, C. G. *Flying Saucers.* New York, NY: MJF Books, 1978.

Kean, Leslie. *UFOs: Generals, Pilots, and Government Officials Go on the Record.* New York, NY: Harmony Books, 2010.

Keel, John A. *The Eighth Tower.* New York, NY: Signet, 1975.

Keel, John A. *The Mothman Prophecies.* New York, NY: Tor, 1991.

Keel, John A. *Our Haunted Planet.* Greenwich, CN: Fawcett Gold Medal, 1971.

Keyhoe, Donald E. *Aliens from Space: The Real Story of Unidentified Flying Objects.* Garden City, NY: Doubleday, 1973.

Keyhoe, Donald. *The Flying Saucers Are Real.* Lexington, KY: CreateSpace, 2012.

Keyhoe, Major Donald E. *The Flying Saucer Conspiracy.* New York, NY: Henry Holt, 1955.

Keyhoe, Major Donald E. *Flying Saucers from Outer Space.* New York, NY: Henry Holt, 1953.

Kinder, Gary. *Light Years: An Investigation into the Extraterrestrial Experiences of Eduard Meier.* New York, NY: Atlantic Monthly Press, 1987.

King, George D. D. *The Flying Saucers: A Report on Flying Saucers, their Crews and their Mission to Earth.* Los Angeles, CA: Aetherius Society, 1964.

Landsburg, Alan and Leonard Nimoy. *In Search of Extraterrestrials.* New York, NY: Bantam Books, 1976.

Larkins, Lisette. *Talking to Extraterrestrials: Communicating with Enlightened Beings.* Charlottesville, VA: Hampton Roads, 2002.

Leir, Roger K. *Alien Implants.* New York, NY: Dell, 2000.

Leonard, George H. *Somebody Else is on the Moon.* New York, NY: Pocket Books, 1976.

Leslie, Desmond and George Adamski. *Flying Saucers Have Landed.* New York, NY: The British Book Centre, 1953.

Lorenzen, Coral E. *Flying Saucers: The Startling Evidence of the Invasion from Outer Space* [original title: *The Great Flying Saucer Hoax*]. New York, NY: Signet, 1966.

Lorenzen, Coral and Jim. *Encounters with UFO Occupants.* New York, NY: Berkley Medallion, 1976.

Lorenzen, Coral and Jim. *Flying Saucer Occupants.* New York, NY: Signet, 1967.

Lorenzen, Jim and Coral. *UFOs Over the Americas.* New York, NY: Signet, 1968.

Lorenzen, Jim and Coral. *UFOs: The Whole Story.* New York, NY: Signet, 1969.

Mack, John E. *Abduction: Human Encounters with Aliens.* New York, NY: Ballantine Books, 1994.

Mack, John E. *Passport to the Cosmos.* New York, NY: Crown, 1999.

Maloney, Mack. *UFOs in Wartime.* New York, NY: The Berkeley, 2011.

Mannion, Michael. *Project Mindshift: The Re-education of the American Public Concerning Extraterrestrial Life, 1947–Present.* New York, NY: M. Evans, 1998.

Marden, Kathleen and Denise Stoner. *The Alien Abduction Files: The Most Startling Cases of Human Alien Contact Ever Reported.* Pompton Plains, NJ: New Page, 2013.

Marrs, Jim. *Alien Agenda: Investigating the Extraterrestrial Presence Among Us.* New York, NY: Harper Collins, 1997.

McCampbell, James M. *Ufology.* Millbrae, CA: Celestial Arts, 1976.

Menger, Howard. *From Outer Space* [original title: *From Outer Space to You.*] New York, NY: Pyramid, 1959.

Menzel, Donald H. and Lyle G. Boyd. *The World of Flying Saucers: A Scientific Examination of a Major Myth of the Space Age.* Garden City, NY: Doubleday, 1963.

Michel, Aimé. *The Truth about Flying Saucers.* New York, NY: Pyramid, 1956.

Mitchell, John. *The Flying Saucer Vision.* New York, NY: Ace, 1967.

Moore, Patrick. *Can You Speak Venusian? A Guide to the Independent Thinkers.* London: Star, 1972.

Moore, William L. *Crashed Saucers: Evidence in Search of Proof.* [no location]: MUFON Symposium Proceedings, 1985.

Moore, William L. and Charles Berlitz. *The Philadelphia Experiment: Project Invisibility.* New York, NY: Grosset & Dunlap, 1979.

Moore, William L. *The Roswell Investigation: New Evidence in the Search for a Crashed UFO.* Prescott, AZ: William L. Moore, 1982.

Moore, William L. and Stanton T. Friedman. *The Roswell Investigation: New Evidence, New Conclusions & The Roswell Incident: Beginnings of the Cosmic Watergate.* Prescott, AZ: William L. Moore, 1982.

Pope, Nick. *Operation Lightning Strike.* London, UK: Simon & Schuster UK, 2000.

Pope, Nick. *The Uninvited: An Exposé of the Alien Abduction Phenomenon.* New York, NY: Dell, 1997.

Randle, Kevin D., Russ Estes, and Wiliam P. Cone. *The Abduction Enigma.* New York, NY: Tom Doherty, 1999.

Randle, Kevin D. *Case MJ-12: The True Story Behind the Government's UFO Conspiracies.* New York, NY: HarperTorch, 2002.

Randle, Kevin D. *A History of UFO Crashes.* New York, NY: Avon, 1995.

Randle, Kevin D. *Invasion Washington: UFOs Over the Capitol.* New York, NY: HarperCollins, 2001.

Randle, Kevin D. *Scientific Ufology.* New York, NY: Avon Books, 1999.

Randle, Kevin D. and Donald R. Schmitt. *The Truth about the UFO Crash at Roswell.* New York, NY: Avon, 1994.

Randle, Kevin D. *The UFO Casebook.* New York, NY: Warner, 1989.

Randle, Kevin D., Capt., U.S.A.F.R., and Donald R. Schmitt. *UFO Crash at Roswell.* New York, NY: Avon, 1991.

Randles, Jenny. *UFO Retrievals: The Recovery of Alien Spacecraft.* London, UK: Blandford, 1995.

Reeve, Bryant and Helen. *Flying Saucer Pilgrimage.* Amherst, WI: Amherst Press, 1957.

Rojas, Alejandro. "Remote Controlled UFO Invasion: RC Aircraft Mistaken for UFOs" in *Open Minds* (February/March). Tempe, AZ: Open Minds Production, 2014.

Ronson, Jon. *The Men Who Stare At Goats.* New York, NY: Simon & Schuster, 2004.

Roseberry, Dinah. *UFO & Alien Management: A Guide to Discovering, Evaluating, and Directing Sightings, Abductions, and Contactee Experiences.* Atglen, PA: Schiffer, 2014.

Ross, Hugh, Samples, Kenneth, and Clark, Mark. *Lights in the Sky & Little Green Men.* Colorado Springs, CO: NavPress, 2002.

Ruppelt, Edward J. *The Report on Unidentified Flying Objects.* Garden City, NY: Doubleday, 1956.

Sachs, Margaret and Ernest Jahn. *Celestial Passengers: UFOs and Space Travel.* New York, NY: Penguin, 1977.

Sacks, Oliver. *Hallucinations.* New York, NY: Random House, 2013.

Sagan, Carl. *Contact.* New York, NY: Pocket Books, 1985.

Salas, Robert and James Klotz. *Faded Giant.* North Charleston, SC: BookSurge, 2005.

Sanderson, Ivan T. *Invisible Residents: The Reality of Underwater UFOs.* Kempton, IL: Adventures Unlimited Press, 1970, 2005.

Sanderson, Ivan T. *Uninvited Visitors: A Biologist Looks at UFOs.* New York, NY: Cowles, 1967.

Saunders, David R. and Harkins, R. Roger. *UFOs? Yes! Where the Condon Committee Went Wrong.* New York, NY: Signet, 1968.

Schulzetenberg, Mark. *Our Lady Comes to Fátima.* St. Paul, MN: Leaflet Missal, 1987.

Scully, Frank. *Behind the Flying Saucers.* New York, NY: Henry Holt, 1950.

Smith, Warren. *UFO Trek.* New York, NY: Zebra, 1976.

Soriano, Frank and Bouck, James. *UFOs Above the Law.* Atglen, PA: Schiffer, 2011.

Spencer, John and Hilary Evans [Editors]. *Phenomenon: Forty Years of Flying Saucers.* New York, NY: Avon, 1988.

Sprague, Ryan. "One by One they Fall" in *Open Minds* (February/March). Tempe, AZ: Open Minds Production, 2014.

Stanton, L. Jerome. *Flying Saucers: Hoax or Reality?* New York, NY: Belmont, 1966.

Steiger, Brad. *Alien Meetings.* New York, NY: Ace, 1978.

Steiger, Brad. *The Fellowship: Spiritual Contact Between Humans and Outer Space Beings.* New York, NY: Ivy, 1988.

Steiger, Brad and Joan Whritenour. *Flying Saucer Invasion Target—Earth.* New York, NY: Award Books, 1969.

Steiger, Brad and Joan Whritenourn. *New UFO Breakthrough.* New York, NY: Award, 1968.

Steiger, Brad, Alfred Bielek, and Sherry Hanson Steiger. *The Philadelphia Experiment & Other UFO Conspiracies.* New Brunswick, NJ: Inner Light, 1990.

Steiger, Brad. *Project Blue Book.* New York, NY: Ballantine, 1976.

Steiger, Brad and Francie. *The Star People.* New York, NY: Berkley, 1981.

Steiger, Brad and Sherry Hansen Steiger. *The UFO Abductors.* New York, NY: Berkley, 1988.

Strieber, Whitley. *Alien Hunter: Underworld.* New York, NY: Tor, 2014.

Strieber, Whitley. *Breakthrough: The Next Step.* New York, NY: HarperPaperbacks, 1995.

Strieber, Whitley. *Communion.* New York, NY: HarperCollins, 1987.

Strieber, Whitley. *Confirmation: The Hard Evidence of Aliens Among Us.* New York, NY: St. Martin's Press, 1998.

Strieber, Whitley. *The Grays.* New York, NY: Tor, 2006.

Strieber, Whitley. *Majestic.* New York, NY: Berkley, 1989.

Strieber, Whitley. *The Secret School: Preparation for Contact.* New York, NY: HarperPaperbacks, 1997.

Strieber, Whitley. *Solving the Communion Enigma*. New York, NY: Penguin, 2011.

Strieber, Whitley. *Transformation: The Breakthrough*. New York, NY: William Morrow, 1988.

Stringfield, Leonard H. *Situation Red: The UFO Siege!* New York, NY: Fawcett Crest, 1977.

Tonnies, Mac. *The Cryptoterrestrials*. San Antonio, TX: Anomalist Books, 2010.

Trench, Brinsley Le Poer. *The Flying Saucer Story*. New York, NY: Ace, 1966.

Trench, Brinsley Le Poer. *Mysterious Visitors: The UFO Story*. New York, NY: Stein and Day, 1971.

Trench, Brinsley Le Poer. *Secret of the Ages: UFO's from Inside the Earth*. New York, NY: Pinnacle, 1974.

Turner, Karla. *Into the Fringe: A True Story of Alien Abduction*. New York, NY: Berkeley, 1992.

Turner, Karla and Ted Rice. *Masquerade of Angels*. Roland, AR: Kelt Works, 1994.

Turner, Karla. *Taken: Inside the Alien-Human Agenda*. Tallahassee, FL: Rose Printing, 1994.

Vallee, Jacque. *Anatomy of a Phenomenon: The Detailed and Unbiased Report of UFOs*. New York, NY: Ace, 1965.

Vallee, Jacque. *Dimensions: A Casebook of Alien Contact*. New York, NY: Ballantine, 1988.

Vallee, Jacque. *Passport to Magonia: From Folklore to Flying Saucers*. Chicago, IL: Henry Regnery, 1969.

Vallee, Jacques. *Revelations: Alien Contact and Human Deception*. New York, NY: Ballantine, 1991.

Vallee, Jacque. *UFO Chronicles of the Soviet Union: A Cosmic Samizdat*. New York, NY: Ballantine, 1992.

Vallee, Jacque and Janine. *The UFO Enigma: Challenge to Science*. New York, NY: Ballantine, 1966.

Walters, Ed and Francis. *UFO Abductions in Gulf Breeze*. New York, NY: Avon Books, 1994.

Walton, Travis. *The Walton Experience*. New York, NY: Berkley Medallion, 1978.

Weldon, John and Levitt, Zola. *UFOs: What on Earth is Happening?* New York, NY: Bantam, 1975.

White, Dale. *Is Something Up There?* New York, NY: Scholastic, 1968.

Wilkins, Harold T. *Flying Saucers on the Attack*. New York, NY: Citadel, 1954.

Wilkins, Harold T. *Flying Saucers Uncensored*. New York, NY: Pyramid, 1955.

Williamson, George Hunt. *Other Tongues, Other Flesh*. London: Neville Spearman, 1965.

Williamson, George Hunt. *Road in the Sky*. London, UK: Futura, 1975.

Wilson, Dr. Clifford. *The Alien Agenda*. New York, NY: Signet, 1988.

Wilson, Dr. Clifford. *UFOs...and Their Mission Impossible*. New York, NY: Signet, 1974.

Wilson, Don. *Secrets of our Spaceship Moon*. New York, NY: Dell, 1979.

Wright, Susan. *UFO Headquarters: Investigations on Current Extraterrestrial Activity*. New York, NY: St. Martin's Paperbacks, 1998.

Yurdozo, Farah. *Love in an Alien Purgatory: The Life and Fantastic Art of David Huggins*. San Antonio, TX: Anomalist, 2009.

Zinsstag, Lou and Timothy Good. *George Adamski: The Untold Story*. Beckenham, Kent, England, UK: CETI Publications, 1983.

Zullo, Allan. *We're Here: True Tales of Alien Encounters*. New York, NY: Scholastic, 1995.

INDEX

JORDAN HOFER is a
MUFON Research Specialist
and author of *Evolutionary
Ufology, Saucerville,* and
*Evidence for the Personhood of
Chimpanzees.*

DAVID BARKER is the
author of *The Revenant of
Rebecca Pascal, Death At The
Flea Circus, and* (with W. H.
Pugmire) *In the Gulfs of Dream
and Other Lovecraftian Tales.*